THE PALACE
1920 - 1

by
Tony Lloyd

Norman: I shall long remember welcoming you into the company in the prop room of the Palace Theatre, Newark-on-Trent, the smell of size and carpenter's glue, the creaking of skips and you locked in the arms of the Prince of Morocco, a married man, ever such a comic sight with his tights round his ankles and you smeared black. I said, "Don't worry, mum's the word, but don't let it happen again." We talked, brewed tea on a paint-stained gas ring, under a photograph of Mr Charles Doran as Shylock, somewhat askew and ever so disapproving. You expressed gratitude and I said, "Now you're one of the family."

THE DRESSER - Ronald Harwood.

Edited by Brien Chitty
PREFACE by NED SHERRIN
Published by Newark & Sherwood District Council
Recreation & Tourism Department
Printed by Technical Print Services Ltd.

ISBN 0 947810 07 2

Illustration Credits

The cover photograph was provided by Newark Museum. The photographs of Cicely Courtneidge, Charles Doran, Alla Nazimova, Anna Pavlova, George Robey, Margaret Rutherford, Sidney Vere Laurie and Donald Wolfit, were supplied by the Raymond Mander & Joe Mitchenson Theatre Collection. The Hamlet playbill, illustrations of George Burnley, advertisements for, an orchestral programme, Robinson Crusoe, Metropolis, Opening of the Palace, Bingo Night, and Cinderella on Ice are from the Advertiser Group Newspapers at Newark Library. The photograph of Gladys Cooper and Ellen Terry in The Bohemian Girl was provided by Brien Chitty and that of Mrs Ernest Randall by James Randall. The Palace Theatre Staff was provided by Cyril Stevenette, and Vina Cooke supplied the photograph of herself with Cliff Richard.

PREFACE

What a valuable revelation to the theatre historian and the local enthusiast is Tony Lloyd's "The Palace Years." Here is a detailed picture of a much loved and valuable theatre and the lightly sketched theatrical background to a by-gone age.

The Palace Newark is famously the cradle of Britain's most challenging classical actor this century, Sir Donald Wolfit (Woolfitt as he was in the Newark beginnings) - the actor for whose performance in Shakespeare I sped with more certainty of excitement than to any other.

And here Wolfit staged one of his early bids for Actor Management, in a week's programme in 1934 when he put on Twefth Night, The Master Builder and Arms and The Man, with a fledgling cast of later luminaries including John Clements, Margaret Rutherford, Dorothy Green, Margaret Webster and Laurier Lister (later a king of intimate revue). Shaw declined to give the venture a blessing, assuring Wolfit that if the citizens of Newark saw his name on the bills they were intelligent enough to know that they were on to a good thing!

But the book is not about Wolfit. It is about the Palace and about change over 52 years. Here you will find out how prices changed. How Emily Blagg built the Palace and quickly got out at a profit. How the bioscope came and went and so did silent films. How live and film entertainment were combined. How Pavlova danced on the stage of the Palace and Frank Forbes Robertson toured there. How Charles Doran reckoned that the manager made a No 1 venue in a No 2 town!

The threat of the Talkies is met and coped with. Variety heralded George Robey, the Prime Minister of Mirth. And lower down the bill Will Fyffe's daughters, The Sisters Fyffe. Fred Carr's Electric Chicken, and Larola "The Funny Man with the Funny ways." Pantomime brought Itrebors Fifteen Wonder Pigeons to Newark and the Palace saw every possible form of entertainment during its struggle to keep going in the fifties and sixties. Rock and Roll and Skiffle came and went bringing Cliff Richard, Billy Fury, Marty Wilde and Wee Willie Harris in its wake. There was wrestling with Leon Arras now better known as Brian Glover and there was Bingo with the invitation, Let Bingo fill your Christmas stocking!

And most dramatically in the seventies there was a battle to save the theatre. Mr Lloyd's book closes triumphantly with a quote from the Advertiser. It's headlines read "CURTAIN UP".

NED SHERRIN

iii

ACKNOWLEDGEMENTS

Without doubt if it had not been for the pages of the Newark Advertiser and Herald newspapers, this book would have been very much the poorer. The local journalists' appetite, including the ubiquitous Chiel, for every tit bit of news and gossip, was insatiable. Reporting all the changes that ensued over the years, they charted the progress of cinema and live theatre in Newark, and provided unique records from which the history of the Palace Theatre Years has, been born.

I shall be eternally grateful to those many local citizens who gave me their time to recall the past. They include Mr and Mrs George Bennett, Ron Chaplin, Pat Coyne, Frank Haxby, Patrick Howell, Harriet Oakes, John Oldham, Roma Parlby, Derek Priestly, Jim Randall, Margery Smithson, Joan Stevenson, Cyril Stevenette, Janet Stevenette, and Vina Cooke of the well known Museum of Dolls and Bygone Childhood. Their invaluable recollections provided vital pieces of the jigsaw and has enriched the history of their beloved Palace.

I thank Ronald Harwood for allowing me to quote from his play "The Dresser", and Margaret Wolfit for permitting quotations from her father's autobiography, "First Interval". Similiarly I am grateful to Brian Hornsey's invaluable "Ninety Years of Cinema in Newark" and the local entertainment index compiled by G. Hemingway.

I was very appreciative that Ned Sherrin agreed to write the Preface, and indebted to Newark and Sherwood District Council for accepting the financial responsibility of Publisher. To Roger Parlby Managing Director and Editor in Chief of Advertiser Group Newspapers, I give my thanks for his support and permitting me to quote extensively from the local press.

I am full of praise for the tireless involvement of Brien Chitty, who has seen this book through the press, to Tim Warner local studies librarian for his professional guidance, and Newark Museum for providing the very rare photograph for our cover design. To the Museum and Library's staff, and to David Piper and the staff and Volunteers of the Palace Theatre I pay tribute for their time given freely in aiding my work and publicising The Palace Years.

To everyone I dedicate this book.

TONY LLOYD

Contents

Illustrations

INTRODUCTION

When the future of the Palace Theatre hangs in the balance, it can be guaranteed to make local headlines. Today it may be the problems of an ageing building, or justifying the amount of subsidy. These problems can pale into insignificance in the shadow of the traumas of the early commercial days. The struggle to survive in the rapidly changing world of entertainment, was dog eat dog in a business highly motivated by profit. All this is revealed in Tony Lloyd's story of the early years of the Palace Theatre.

It became clear as research progressed, that the volume of information Tony was gathering would far exceed our capacity in time and budget. It was imperative therefore to have a cut off point which logically is 1972, when the town acquires the premises, and the period of commercial enterprise comes to an end.

Information beyond this period is filed for a future historian, who must have the same tenacity and resilience that Tony produced. He beavered away, spending countless hours at Newark Library, sifting through pages of the local newspapers for any report of the Palace, and those that worked behind the scenes or appeared on the stage. His many interviews with local people has also been thorough, but again he came away with far more information than could be used today.

Theatre Research is an ongoing job. For three years Tony toiled with unswerving dedication, uncovering the forgotten history of Newark's Palace Theatre. I hope that there will be some civic pride in this publication, and that someone will come forward in due course to add to his work. The reward for Tony's diligence is this publication, of which I am privileged to be involved.

BRIEN CHITTY

THE PALACE YEARS
(1920-1972)

Chapter 1

IN THE BEGINNING - 1900-1920

1.   Setting the Stage:
     Buskers, Barnstormers and the Bioscope

By the opening decade of the twentieth century industrial production had reached a new peak. If production was to materially increase, it was necessary to view the populace in a different light. From being just a necessity of producing wealth for the employer, the workers were to be regarded as customers. Beginning in the USA, a bombardment of advertisements began a journey into leisure expenditure. The world of mass entertainment was one important result of this trend over the succeeding decades.

In those early days in Newark entertainment, excluding public houses, was sparse. Cinema and radio did not exist. A family piano and the human voice were the height of attainment on special occasions. This lack of entertainment had for centuries been relieved by companies of travelling entertainers with varying degrees of competence.Frank Benson gave performances of "As You Like It" in the grounds of Handley House in August 1895, whilst Donald Wolfit experienced the "Buskers" and "Barnstormers" of the annual May Fair. His one visit to the play "Maria Marten And The Murder In The Red Barn" in a tent was not good. "I was quite overpowered by the strong smell of humanity in the tent". Lord George Sanger's Circus visited the town annually, and was watched "shivering with excitement" as it proceeded towards town.

A new form of travelling show arrived during this decade. Although Newark had no theatre, a twice weekly travelling bioscope show began to visit the Corn Exchange. Sir Donald reflects that this was "where I saw the earliest of films, on those occasions when the bioscope did not break down and our money was returned". Unreliability was not the only problem of those early cinematograph machines. The materials were quite liable to burst into flames. The frequent fires that occurred led to The Cinematograph Act 1909. This forced exhibitors to provide a fireproof projection area and sufficient emergency exits. The result was that existing premises were refurbished and adapted. In Newark these were: The Corn Exchange, The Picturedome and Beaumond Hall.

The Corn Exchange, Castlegate, was transformed into the Cinematograph Hall by Messrs. Gale & Company, who obtained the lease of the property from the 6th September 1913. Previously cinema shows and "Variety" had been run on an irregular basis. In these early days films were quite short and variety artists provided an opportunity to change the cinematographic reels as well as being an attraction in their own right. The refurbished Corn Exchange continued into the first World War. However, Messrs. Gale & Company had also taken an interest in the syndicate set up by Emily Blagg, to erect and run a new cinema, which was to be known as the Kinema. Messrs. Gale soon withdrew from the area leaving the Corn Exchange on the periphery of the entertainment scene in Newark.

The Skating Rink/New Theatre/Picturedrome was born out of a skating boom. As interest quickly declined the proprietors adopted Cinema with Variety. In fact the last independent owners abbreviated their policy, in their name, CINEVARS. Donald Wolfit recalled the Picturedrome in it's early days:

> "Before the war some businessmen in the town had built a tin roofed skating rink, which was at first a sensation but later fell on bad days and was closed. Then a stage was built at one end and the place showed films, changing the programme twice weekly. Later came the addition of Music Hall turns, usually three in number each week. I had on two occasions been allowed to visit the Music Hall at Nottingham to see George Robey. This considerably raised my standard of appreciation and I was not slow to realise that the bulk of variety turns were of poor quality indeed. The jokes were coarse and smutty but we were in the middle of a great war. The town was packed with troops and the lowest tastes were catered for. I do remember Will Hay and his act was as amusing and free from vulgarity as ever it was but drew as great applause as the cheap and nasty comedians."

Beaumond Hall Cinema emerged from the old Cartergate Drill Hall in 1914. It was a small cinema circa 300 seats and although initially showing variety amongst films, it soon exclusively concentrated upon "the best pictures always."

Once the premises had been prepared and the equipment installed, the new management, in this infant industry, had to decide what policy should be implemented to fill their cinemas. In the early days much experimentation occurred. There were great financial opportunities arising from these technological advances. Outsiders were not slow to seek the means to enter this new arena.

One such remarkable local entrepreneur was Emily Blagg who decided that the best way to enter the business was the creation of a purpose built cinema. In fact she came to build two such palaces of entertainment and the battle for Newark's paying customers was enjoined. But let us remember that although many opportunities existed a substantial amount of capital had to be found and used before any income was forthcoming. It was quite possible that the picture-going enthusiasm would fade as quickly as the roller skating craze.

2.   Enter Emily Blagg

With the stage set for her appearance into show business a brief picture of her life will aid in understanding this multi-faceted and liberated lady.

Born Emily Stevens in 1863, her formative years are largely unknown. Coming to Newark with her family in 1883 this statuesque, vivacious and confident young lady, with a mane of thick brunette hair, was employed by Cooper & Co., for the next 20 years. Her excellent taste for colours made her a valuable employee and she became a buyer and demonstrator for the firm. She often travelled to Paris to buy the best silks for this high class firm. She would be able to make contacts with the best Newark families. She never seemed to have had any impediments to self progress in an age when women only received the vote in 1918. In fact the professions were closed to most educated women and many were occupied with charities or tending the home, which was the focus of their being. Working class women were either engaged in manual labour or excessive child bearing. Emily was different.

When she left Coopers in 1903, her next career was that of speculative builder! In 1905, at the age of 42, she married Mr. William Thomas Blagg, a local butcher, who was some years her junior. He died before Emily without issue. The report of Emily's death carried a fitting tribute of a building estate pioneer in Newark and reveals that she was the subject of an article in a national daily newspaper. The writer calling her The Lady Builder. To detail her progress constitutes a considerable amount of work in just 17 years. She purchased a brickworks site in Cross Street with a siding onto the main LNER railway. Although not specifically catalogued it is thought she built a row of houses in Massey Street for her workers. Although the area has extensive new buildings and demolition has occurred the Blagg bricks are quite distinctive. Her first acknowledged site was The Park, which she developed into a residential district and was considered the most artistic in town. This took 3 years to complete. About this time a colliery at Dinnington, in Yorkshire, was being built and Emily built a large number of houses there. Her next project was the Lime Grove Estate. This estate was to provide much needed houses for the working classes at reasonable rents. On the London Road corner of this estate was built her future home - The Lodge, 131 Lime Grove. She had an enviable reputation for success. At this point she built the Kinema and her Palace.

I now revert back to the events leading to both theatres. Her years after the Palace will be chronicled in a later chapter.

With Emily Blagg's speculative inclinations it could have been no surprise that her attention would be drawn to the emerging entertainment industry in Newark. People wanted cinemas so why should she not provide them. *The Newark Herald* revealed the intention of this established business-woman on the 28th December 1912.

"NEW PICTURE PALACE FOR NEWARK - We understand that Mrs. Blagg has purchased Messrs Ford's old carriage works, opposite The Rutland Arms Hotel, Barnbygate, which she intends to demolish and build on the site a first class Picture Palace, with all the latest improvements. A special feature is to be made of the seating accommodation, to ensure the comfort of the patrons. The work will commence immediately."

This news of the establishment of a brand new, up-to-date cinema, in a good location, practically next door to the other cinemas, must have given the proprietors in Newark a somewhat disquieting breakfast. Soon on the heels of this headline came another (*The Newark Advertiser*, 8th January 1913).

"A NEW PICTURE THEATRE - Definite steps have been taken towards the project of a new picture theatre for Newark. It transpires that a syndicate in which Mrs. Emily

Blagg, Messrs Gale & Co., and others, are said to be members, have purchased the house and premises in Barnbygate, formerly occupied by the late Mr. Ford, as a residence and coach building shops. A picture theatre was formerly proposed on the site but the plans submitted were not in accordance with the by-laws and accordingly were not then approved. 'In the present instance, a block of cottage properties belonging to Mr. Z. Johnson, Baldertongate, and known as Coopers Yard was also acquired by Mrs. Blagg last Friday. This property backs up to the Barnbygate Premises and also has a good frontage to Baldertongate. When all the buildings are demolished there will be opened out an attractive site with frontages to two principal thoroughfares'."

It had been thought that both articles were reporting the same event. However, it seems from the detailed articles and the business sense of Emily Blagg that she was attempting to build a cinema solely on the Ford Carriage works. When permission was denied, owing to non compliance of the plans with the by-laws, she swiftly obtained the financial support of friends and Gale & Co., who must have felt threatened as prospective proprietors of the Corn Exchange, to extend the scheme over a larger area with natural exits at both ends.

The article continues

"The speculation is a bold one, as the purchase prices are said to be in the region of £3,000, when the cost of clearing the site has been added. This betokens great confidence in the picture business of the future. Messrs Gale & Co., it will be recognised, are the lesees of the Corn Exchange, Newark and are adepts at the picture show business. It would appear that in due course the Corn Exchange business will be transferred to the new theatre. The work of demolition is to be commenced at once."

The plans were duly passed by the Council. To finance the new theatre (The Kinema) a company called Newark Kinemas was floated on the 30th April, 1913, in the value of £6,000 in one pound shares, the head office being that of Messrs Gale & Co., London. An experienced architect was engaged. Messrs Wright & Renshaw entered a successful tender of £3,275.17s. and by August 1913 work had begun. The Kinema opened on the 20th December 1913, having been superintended by Emily Blagg.

After this huge project, it would not have been expected that any other project would be envisaged until the large expenditure had been recouped by the proprietors. However, they had not reckoned on the restless Emily Blagg. She had experienced the planning and building of one cinema and learned greatly. She was now ready to build a Palace for Newark.

3.   The Chauntry Ashes

As soon as 26th May 1914, she was actively present at an auction at Messrs E. Bailey & Sons Saleroom where several lots of local property were submitted to auction. The principal lot was the historic freehold Queen Anne residence known as 'the Chauntry' with it's panelled oak rooms and other notable features. Mr. Bailey, who conducted the sale, said the idea was that if they could not treat that night they would at once start to dismantle the place and clear it away. Bidding commenced at £2,000 and at £3,000 Emily Blagg occupied the field but at £3,100 the property was withdrawn. The house was then put up by itself, but was withdrawn at £2,200.

Whether this occasion was Emily Blagg's first interest in The Chauntry is not known but certainly she was always on the lookout for good sites for sale, and later used auction houses for the sale of her own products. She cannot have ignored this huge property with extensive grounds, including a deer park, which had seen better days. Even 75 years after it's demise many local people still say it's demolition was a huge mistake and that this beautiful and historical building, one of the treasurers of Newark, was allowed to be purchased for demolition and the whole site re-developed, was not popular.

An article in the Newark Advertiser dated 16th April 1919, gives an excellent look at its past. The history of the Chauntry site stems back to a medieval building erected by Dame Alice Fleming to perpetuate the memory of her husband, Alan Fleming, to whose memory there is also in the Parish Church a famous medieval brass. The Flemings flourished in Newark in the 14th Century and were wool merchants 'brought over' from Flanders. Newark being at the time the centre of a large wool growing district and cloth was made in the vicinity. 'The Chauntry house was dedicated to the use of the priests who celebrated at the numerous altars in the church'. It was a clerical social club and a forerunner of the modern church house, a small chamber being reserved for each priest as well as a larger common room. The special function was to sing Mass for the soul of the founder of the Chantry and other departed relatives. Newark was rich in the number of these chantries in the 14th and 15th Centuries. On their dissolution by Henry VIII in 1550 the house was purchased by William Breton and Ambrose Nicholas, both of London.

It afterwards came into the possession of the Leck family, by one of the descendants of whom it was sold in 1681 to Samuel Foster of Woodborough, who rebuilt and reconstructed the Chauntry as a fine specimen of Queen Anne's reign, highly enriched in the Palladian style with a sumptuous interior. Families came and went, the last in 1911, when a huge sale of contents was made over several days.

On 14th February 1912 *The Advertiser* featured an advertisement headed 'Chauntry To Let Unfurnished' and it read

"the house is full of beautiful old oak carving and panelling and contains 4 reception rooms, large hall and lobby, 10 bed and dressing rooms, bathroom, good stabling for 7 horses with coach house, harness room and outbuildings, good garden with 3 glass houses and park containing about 4 acres."

Apparently no tenant was found. Hence the auction attended by Emily Blagg on 26th May 1914. The house was withdrawn at auction and nothing could be done until the Great War was concluded in 1918. During the war the property was used as officers' quarters. Mrs. Blagg was offered the site and house. This time she and the vendors reached an agreement. An item in the *Newark Advertiser* on 8th January 1919, on page five, revealed that

"speculation as to the fate of the Chauntry, Appletongate, can now be set at rest. It was sold yesterday to a private purchaser who we understand intends to develop it as a building estate."

On 26th February 1919 the *Advertiser* gave details revealing the new owner:-

"NEW STREET FOR NEWARK - Mrs. Blagg of Lime Grove, Newark, having recently purchased the excellent building site in Appletongate, known as the Chauntry, has already got out a scheme for developing some of the land which includes a new street. The plans have recently been before the Council and Mrs. Blagg has also asked the Corporation to rename Bede House Lane. The houses, which are to be villas, will be erected parallel to those in Magnus Street and will extend through the Chauntry estate from Appletongate to Priory Road and will face Beacon Hill road. Provision is also being made for the erection of a commodious comfortable and up to date theatre, the entrance to which will adjoin the Magnus Buildings in Appletongate."

So Emily had finally secured the property after 5 years waiting. It appears that from later debates by the Council, on the Chauntry site that at least one other person had tried to secure the site for the benefit of the community. This was revealed by the *Newark Advertiser* when reporting the meeting of the Newark Town Council on 6th May 1919. A paragraph headed 'The Mayor's Intention'. The Major Alderman Mr. W. E. Knight said "that he hoped this site (the Chauntry) would have been secured for the town and he went so far on his own behalf as to make an offer for it, intending to give it to the town. The matter was in hand but someone came forward and outbid him and he lost it."

Emily Blagg's plans had caused 'considerable adverse comment'. The report in the *Newark Advertiser* 16th April 1919 states

"The Chauntry house is now in the hands of the housebreakers and that spectacle of the gutted interior of what was until recently one of the architectural features of Newark is giving occasion for much adverse comment, regret, and reproach on the part of townspeople and visitors. The opinion seems to be widespread that the Chauntry should have been purchased by the Corporation and retained as a museum with its ample grounds utilised as pleasure gardens for the inhabitants."

With the building demolished the Council finally rejected any action to interfere. Dr. Stallard, while sympathising with fellow councillors, stated that "it was a little late in the day." Anxious to avoid any unpopularity Emily Blagg had made a verbal offer through the Borough Surveyor to the Corporation of the remaining portion of the Chauntry land 'at what it cost' (*N.A.* 28.5.19). As this was quite informal and no data was given, the Committee thought Mrs. Blagg should be asked to put her offer into writing. Knowing her to be a skilled negotiator, realising that cost has many interpretations and a reply was required in two weeks, no further action was taken. Ironically Emily Blagg never built on the site. This was due to the fact that her capital was tied up in Blagg & Johnson. Her brickyard was built over and the business took a long time to pay its way. I am sure that if she had chosen to develop the Chauntry site in 1920 rather than finance Mr. Johnson, she would have been far happier.

An article entitled "Did they jerrybuild in Queen Anne's time?", revealed that the house was on the point of collapse. After paying a visit to the Chauntry house now in process of demolition and making a close examination of the mansion a heap of debris in the centre of the building was explained by the foreman housebreaker.

"On Saturday night a couple of hundredweight of bricks pushed off a chimney stack on to the floor of the top room, resulting in the collapse of the ceiling through worm eaten beams and joists. The mass crashed through the lower floor and brought both to the ground. The great majority of the oak beams were worm eaten and rotten. Some beams bear evidence that they were installed before the Queen Anne House was built from numerous mortice holes which do not fit with the present building and the tenons are mere shadows of their former selves."

The correspondent damningly ends

"while it was a complete whole it held together but when any part had to take the least stress it failed. It seems clear in my view that it is a good job for the town the building was not purchased to keep it, as sooner or later it would have proved a veritable death trap."

From this point the building of THE PALACE went unhindered. Emily was not only the entrepreneur but supplier of bricks, Clerk of Works, Quantity Surveyor and Supervisor of the various contractors. She kept a close eye on all operations throughout the building of Newark's Housing estates and theatres. Arriving on her bicycle, her ample proportions would be seen climbing all over the scaffolding, even to the top most roof sections. She inspected, innovated, instructed and disciplined the work force and even manually added to the building. She was then aged 57 years.

Although many Chauntry fittings had been sold prior to the Great War and several 'souvenirs' were liberated during the war, the residue was disposed of behind the high fence, by Mrs. Blagg. Some fittings were sold or given away while a great deal of material was used in the building of the Palace. Mr. A. Priestley, who was experienced in Theatre and Cinema organisation and a Mrs. Kirk were employed some months prior to the opening of the Palace cleaning bricks amongst other tasks. So it is highly probable that a fair amount of the Palace brickwork was scavenged from the demolished Chauntry as were three doors and who knows what else. One of these doors probably exists today. The other two formed the entrance from the foyer into the cinema until 1974 when the Punch and Judy room, comprising of a bar, cafeteria and lounge, was created out of the back stalls.

By May 1920 the building was nearing completion. However, the odd wag such as Yorick in his gossip column could not resist a dig against the general euphoria by announcing the following in the *Newark Advertiser* 20th May 1920.

"The rumours about the new Palace being pulled down are officially denied."

4.   Theatre or Cinema

On 23rd June 1920 the Newark Advertiser, with a heading 'The Palace Theatre Nearing Completion', has given a masterly description of the Palace. I can do no better than produce it in full. It must have excited the populace who arrived in their droves at the opening.

"Newark is about to receive a notable addition to its places of entertainment in the Palace Picture Theatre, which has been raised upon the old Chauntry site. It used to be a reproach that our townsmen had to go to Nottingham for amusement, and this was not good for the trade of the town. At least in the matter of Cinemas the town is well off and will now be possessed of as palatial a Picture House as can be found anywhere. No money has been spared in its construction. It can vie with anything Nottingham or other cities within reach can offer. The new owner of the Theatre already controls elite and popular theatres in Sheffield, which have commanded the confidence of patrons and extraordinary success. We are assured by the proprietor that the class of pictures will be of such a high-class character that any man can take either his ladyfriend or (if married) his wife and children. Everything that art and mechanics can supply for the perfection of the projection of the pictures has been procured. Not only will the subject matter be right but the photography in its light and shade, clear definition and detail will be unsurpassed. The luxurious finish of the theatre, comfortable seating and unimpeded view of the screen from every seat in the large hall will ensure the satisfaction and enjoyment of patrons. The building is in the Byzantine style with its imposing facade to Appletongate. A feature of the structure are the minarets which give it an Oriental touch and are unique in this neighbourhood. There is a spacious foyer giving entrance to the main hall and the grand staircase for the balcony. Here tall palms and lounge chairs are dispersed and the ticket boxes are tucked modestly away in the corners. This noble entrance prepares the visitor for the charm and beauty of the interior decorations.

Imposing as the theatre is in its sweep and dimensions as viewed from the outside, the impression from the inside is still more pleasing. The artistic architectural features have been accentuated by the masterly work of Mr. Lazzarini, of Lenton, Nottingham, whose fibrous plaster work is a notable feature of the Palace from his own designs, and carried out entirely by his firm. The ceiling is slightly cambered and is in the French style of the Louis XIV period, the ornamental floral design showing up in bold relief. The gracefulness of this work and the wall panelling show the highest artistic perceptive excellence. The stage, which has a depth of 48 feet from front to back, could accommodate the best touring Theatrical Companies, but will not now be utilised.

Mr. Lazzarini's work on the proscenium surround and the balcony front is strikingly beautiful. The former is left pure white and the latter relieved by Dresden blue tints giving an appearance of the famous pottery. On the walls the panelling is bold, filled in with tapestry designs and pierced by the chaste electric fittings. There is a blue painted Dado round the walls, whilst the trellised ceiling and borders are picked out in light primrose tints.

The comfort of patrons is assured by the excellent work of Messrs. Beck and Windybank, Birmingham. The seats are all upholstered in peacock blue plush, and so excellently arranged, in alternate rows, that people will have an uninterrupted view of the exhibition by looking between the seats instead of the usual method of gazing, with discomfort, over one another's heads. The decorations tone with the upholstery. Luxurious carpets, soft to the tread and pleasing to the eye are laid on the stalls and gangways, special attention being paid to the lounge, in which teas will be served. The balcony promenade is an enterprising innovation which will be exceedingly popular. There are two emergency exits from the balcony and the main staircase and in the main hall eight exits.

Special attention has been paid to the ventilating system so that the interior may be cool in summer and warm in winter. Fresh air is circulated into the building during the summer months direct, but in the winter it is warmed first. There are three large extractors to carry out the impure air.

The operating room is designed on the best possible principle. It is fireproof. It has a steel roof and is lined with cement concrete. The automatic shutters over the apertures will make it impossible for a fire to spread. Provision has been made for three machines - two films and one lantern. There are two separate lighting supplies - electricity and gas. The electric power will be supplied by two 45 h.p. Crossley engines, two dynamos and storage battery. The gas is from the Town supply.

There is every modern convenience for theatre-goers, as supplied in the best London and provincial houses of entertainment. Cloak rooms and lavatories, as well as a patent check ticket at the two booking offices in the entrance hall. Mr. J. W. Armstrong, the manager, has an office next the lounge and refreshment room, where he can be consulted at any moment. Seats can be booked in advance between 10 and 12 and 2 and 4 p.m. each day.

The structural works were carried out by Mr. A. Wright, Newark; electrical work by Messrs. Harrison and Co., Newark; heating by Messrs. Goodacre, Glover and Butler, London-road, Nottingham; plaster and fancy decorating by Mr. Lazzarini, Nottingham; furnishing and seating by Messrs. Beck and Windybank, Birmingham; painting and decorating, Mr. W. S. Heading, Newark; plumbing, etc., Mr. Smith. Mrs. Blagg has been in control of all the operations.

Mr. B. Raphael, popular in music circles, particularly in Scotland, where he has charge of a large orchestra, will be the conductor of an excellent string band consisting of piano, two violins, 'cello, bass, cornet, clarinet and other instruments as accommodation will permit. The best class music will be discoursed, and by request, special items will be played.

Miss Ralph, well-known in Newark for her work in connection with the catering at the Y.W.C.A., at Northgate House, will supervise the cafe and tea rooms and lounge. It is intended to open the cafe at 10.30 each morning until 10 p.m. in order to cater for visitors and townspeople who desire morning coffee and light refreshments."

Even 75 years from its opening it is asked whether the Palace was built as a theatre or a cinema. I am sure that the building was meant to be a wonder, a Palace, a pinnacle of excellence to be admired from afar. It was also perhaps a twist of conscience? Was it to be a phoenix arising from the flames of the demolished Chauntry building which was still being mourned?

I think Emily, as a practical person, decided that the diversification of uses of a building would produce wider attractions, survive longer and be a better selling property.

In fact at the end of the second paragraph of the preceding description of the Palace theatre it outlines the capacity of the stage but adds "the stage could accomodate the best touring Theatrical Companies but will not now be utilized."

Following the comprehensive details of The Palace as, released in the Advertiser above, large advertisements appeared on the front page of the local newspapers on the week preceding the opening on Monday 5th July 1920. It outlined the timing and days of the shows, booking arrangements for the Balcony seats and the function of the Cafe & Lounge, which was to serve Tea, Coffee and minerals and light refreshments from 10.30 a.m. daily. This was to be the start of many large front page advertisements to be placed by the Palace management. The result was that by opening night Newark's appreciation was shown.

> "Long before half past six - the time of the first performance - a large number of folk formed a queue in Appleton Gate. The scene was quite novel and the atmosphere seemed to have been suddenly changed to that which hovers round a London Theatre.
>
> Patrons were marshalled by a smartly uniformed commissionaire and tickets purchased in the artistically arranged foyer which is exquisitely carpeted and overhung with baskets of flowers. The interior of the house presented a pretty picture under the soft lights of many globes each hidden by a different coloured shade."

The Advertiser gives its verdict as follows:

> "It was no idle platitude to say that the new Palace Theatre has been warmly welcomed by Newark. It's presence in our midst is recognised as an acquisition to the town, an artistic possession and a dignified home of the silent drama. Its advent is illustrative of the town's bid for progress, and townsfolk are enabled to patronize a theatre which compares most favourably with house de luxe in the largest citities of the country. Nothing has been forgotten in a modern scheme of design and the wealth of beauty and tasteful details evoked much eulogistic comment."

As the 1300 seats were filled, Chiel the local columnist was escorted to his seat where all the rows were lettered. "You are in 'ELL' Mr. Chiel" the usherette stated. In fact he was near to cinema heaven. Films had improved from the early pioneering days. A class of professionals now ruled. However several films were needed to comprise an evening's show and other cinemas were still a mixture of variety turns and films. The Palace opted for the best of films, surroundings, music and food. The main opening production was "King Solomon's Mines" a film version of H. Rider Haggard's classic novel. Also in the programme were one or two

12

Monday, Tuesday, and Wednesday.

SPECIAL ATTRACTION.

CHARLES RAY

IN THE DELIGHTFUL COMEDY DRAMA

BILL HENRY.

Billy Henry Jenkins, country lad, failing to amass a fortune selling electric vibrators, goes to work as night clerk in a small town hotel conducted by his uncle. Lela Mason comes from Keokuk, Iowa, to claim a farm left by a deceased relative, and finds it to be worthless swamp land. She is in deep distress, and Bill determines to help her. He wins enough money in a poker game to buy the farm from the girl. Then oil is discovered on the property. Bill urges a real estate agent to sell the property for him and turn over the proceeds to Lela as an additional bequest from her uncle. The agent plans to annex both girl and money, and thrilling events follow.

Pathe Gazette, the Latest News in Pictures. Pictorial Gazette.

Down where the Yankee Bacon grows. Ju-Jitsu. The Duck Family at home. On the slopes of Mount Pelouze.
Four more Competitors in the Beauty Competition.

PRICE OF A GOOD SNEEZE.

Fox Comedy.

PIPE DREAMS & PRIZES.

A 2-Reel Vitagraph Comedy.

MUSICAL PROGRAMME.

Overture	"Le Petit Duc"	Ch. Lecocq
Intermede	"Cout prez de vous"	G. Krier
Valse Berceuse	"Mondaine"	A. Box
Gavotte	"Gavotte ex Beaux Atours"	G. Monchet
Selection	"Le Cloches de Corneville"	R. Planquette
Tango	"El Opera"	G. Laufveryns
Valse-Impromptu	"Rose d'Amour"	G. Krier
Selection	"Don Cezar de Bazan"	J. Massenet
Intermezzo	"Danse sous la Feuillee"	G. Razigade
Marche	"Pour le Drapeau"	G. Krier
Fox Trot	"Yankyano"	D. Comer
Fox Trot	"Top Hole"	Y. Hickey

Thursday, Friday, and Saturday.

THE FAMOUS DRURY LANE MELO-DRAMA.

The White Heather.

BY CECIL RALEIGH AND HENRY HAMILTON.

This great Drury Lane Melo-drama is transformed into a visualisation of scenic charm with consummate skill. The photography, as also the acting, is admirable and many of the scenes, including the great struggle between men on the bottom of the Ocean, the wreckage at their feet, the fish all around them and the bubbles of escaping air—a unique and most thrilling spectacle—make this one of the most stirring and realistic achievements ever screened.

Pathe Gazette, the Latest News in Pictures.

STRUCK OUT.

Comedy.

HE MARRIED HIS WIFE.

Q.E.D., a 2-Reel Comedy—One Long Laugh.

MUSICAL PROGRAMME.

Overture	"Le Barbier de Seville"	G. Rossini
Piece Caracteristique	"Les Clairs de Lune,"	C. Kooshlin
Chanson	"Pauvre Fous"	D. Tagliafico
Selection	"Il Trovatore"	G. Verdi
Valse	"Lettre Tendre"	A. Box
Gavotte	"Cherubin"	J. Clerice
Selection	"Thais"	J. Massenet
Romance	"Stanza"	G. Razigade
Ballet	"Milenka (a) Kermessé Flamande"	
	(b) "Serenade"	J. Blockx
Marche	"Marche des Sous-offs"	E. Faidoy
Fox Trot	"1920 Jazz"	H. Darewski
Genre	"Danse du Diable"	G. Krier

THE PALACE ORCHESTRA.—Musical Director, B. Raphael.

The Management invite requests for the playing of particular items of music.

The Popular Rendezvous—CAFE AND LOUNGE.

MORNING COFFEES, AFTERNOON TEAS (dainty Cakes a speciality), Ices, &c.
Writing Room and Smoking Room Now Open.

Prices of Admission:

Balcony 1/8, Tax 4d., 2/-. Saloon 1/-, Tax 3d., 1/3. Pit 7d., Tax 2d., 9d.

Children under 12, Half-price—Tuesdays, Wednesdays and Fridays, also Matinees:
Balcony, 9d., Tax 3d., 1/-; Saloon 7d., Tax 2d., 9d.; Pit 4½d., Tax 1½d., 6d.
Seats for Balcony booked in advance 3d. extra. Box Office open 10—12, 2—4.

One of the many ambitious orchestral programmes

reelers support features. A reel usually lasted ten minutes. On the opening night the supports were Fatty Arbuckle Comedian in 'The Garage', Pathe Gazette Pictorial (the latest news in pictures) and a topical film dealing with the Cinema world called 'Movie Chats'.

A seven piece Palace Orchestra under the conductorship of Mr. B. Raphael accompanied the film and gave a full programme of popular classical music including requests. An excellent quality restaurant cafe provided refreshment for patrons and a high class venue for the non cinemagoer. Patrons attended in formal dress. One surviving patron remembers the excellent beverages partaken by an immaculately dressed and numerous clientele, and the orchids on the ladies evening dresses.

5. Emily Sells Out

This theatre was a great success but never rested on its laurels. The management was skilled, professional and experienced. So who was running the Palace?

Emily Blagg had sold out before the building was operational. During the building of the Palace the uneven bricks used to build the Palace had given great problems when crisp sharp corners of quality buildings were required. The unevenness resulted from non standardised moulds. Mr. Frank Milhill Johnson an Australian expert on metal products was consulted. He recommended a metal angle bead, which when enclosed around the brick corner and rendered, produced an immaculate corner. So impressed was Emily that she raised sufficient monies including selling the Palace to build a factory concentrating upon innovative high quality metal products. This rashness can be explained by the character of Johnson who was a superb raconteur brimming full of new ideas. He has been described as 'gorgeous' by a very level headed lady. He was one of the first owners of a motor scooter. The local children awaited his arrival every day on his machine wearing a trilby hat. An article in the *Newark Herald* on 16 April 1921 which must have been an interview with Johnson, concerning the new metal pipe factors at Newark shows the breadth of his inventive mind. However he suddenly left the area and the firm of Blagg & Johnson. All sorts of rumours exist. It is very unusual that Johnson although a partner is not named as a share holder. His loss left Emily Blagg in an invidious position. She knew little about high technology ironwork and had invested heavily in the project. The factory was built over her brickworks. By mid February 1922 she appointed Mr. Alan Menmuir as works manager. A superb engineer, a brilliant mathematician and an expert designer of slide rules, he lifted the floundering firm to a position of respectability, despite his junior status. It must have been galling for Emily Blagg to be reliant upon Menmuir for the recovery of her fortune. It is no wonder that she railed at her monies being tied up and an absence of dividends until 1931. I have heard from separate eye witnesses that she drank to excess. She died 7th April 1935 leaving her shares to her brother and sisters. Ironically as joint manager and director on Emily's death, Alan Menmuir then more than trebled the firm's profits. F. Mcneill & Co., took over the company in January 1938, but the name of Blagg & Johnson remained and the sign can be seen illuminated from the old A17 road down Beacon Hill to your left. They are still producing quality metal products.

Both the Palace and the Kinema management consisted of professionals in the cinema industry and local business men who believed in Emily Blagg's business sense. With her sale of the Palace a consortium developed. On 14th August 1920 *The Newark Herald* mentioned that

"a company is about to be formed for the purpose of purchasing two large modern Cinema Houses at Newark. Mr. Philip K. Wake JP Chairman of Carlton Main Colliery Ltd., is to be chairman. Mr. Isaac Graham a director of Star Picture House & Central Pictures Ltd., the managing director. Mr. W. H. Ravenscroft Managing Director of the Cinema House Company is also joining the Board. The fact that these well known gentlemen are connected with the new company is in itself a security for its future success. Two local gentlemen are understood to be joining the Board of Directors."

On 1st September 1920 a prospectus was issued. Mr. Ravenscroft was the Vendor and the capital needed to be raised to acquire as a going concern the newly refurbished Kinema and the Palace was £55,000. It was an excellent deal. Even allowing for only one-third of the seats to be occupied a net trading profit of £12,941 per annum would be realised. A 10% dividend would account for £5,500 leaving £7,441 to provide for depreciation, renewals, directors remuneration and secretary's salary.

The local Directors were J. H. W. Ford Antiques Dealer and J. E. Oldham Confectioner & Caterer.

The registered office was to be 54 Bank St., Sheffield. The address of the Secretary incorporated accountant E. Ransom Harrison. This was how Newark Cinemas Ltd. was created.

At this point in time Newark possessed in addition to the Palace and the Kinema two other cinemas; Beaumont Hall with a 300 seating capacity which provided the best films while the Picturedrome presented variety and films in competition with the Kinema. By April 1923 both theatres had disappeared. Newark Cinemas Ltd. purchased the Picturedrome in April 1921 and Beaumond Hall in April 1922, after a period of active competition.

Chapter 2

BIRTH OF NEWARK CINEMAS LTD. 1920-30

1.   Cine - Variety - A Commercial Enterprise

From the outset Newark Cinemas Ltd. set out to maximise income from the various activities of the Palace. Both J.W. Armstrong (Manager) and Miss Ralph (Cafeteria Manageress) were to prove superb acquisitions for the Company, remaining there until into the nineteen thirties.

To the right of the entrance were 2 small shops for hire. Mr. E. J. Twydell opened 'The Palace Tobacco & Cigar Stores'. The advertisement states

"Mr. E. J. Twydell has opened the above adjoining The Palace Theatre with a large selection of tobaccos, cigarettes, cigars and all kinds of smokers requisites."

There is no documentation regarding the tenants of the other shop. But it is well known that the shops were regularly tenanted. This income when added to profits from the cafeteria and other miscellaneous income of both Palace and Kinema theatres amounted to £1,250. This represented about 5% of the expected total income of the group.

Upstairs behind the Balcony lay a large area of space which apart from the Cafeteria was available for all types of promotions throughout the years. Offices were provided for both the manager and the cafeteria manageress Miss Ralph. Several adverts acclaimed specific advantages of the Palace 'Cafe and Lounge'. 'During performances the orchestra can be heard distinctly in the Cafe'. (28/7/20 *N.A.*)'The ventilation system installed in this theatre enables the atmosphere to be completely changed every five minutes'. 'This building is kept scrupulously clean and the acme of comfort is thus assured to our patrons'. 'The Cafe and Lounge possesses a writing room, smoke room, Public telephone and cloakroom'.

The first innovation of the new management was that 'a special Orchestra will play in the Cafe on Mondays, Tuesdays, Thursdays and Fridays between 4 p.m. and 5.30 p.m. A special feature will be made of all the latest Dance Music and songs'. (*N.A.* 29/9/20) To further publicise the catering facility from 13/10/20 an offer of a free afternoon tea was made to Saturday matinee balcony patrons. Yorick the light gossip columnist reports that the offer was so popular that the food stores were so depleted that the evening dinner patrons could not be provided with soup. The promotional offer was withdrawn on 27/10/20 *(N.A.)*

Although the films were silent music abounded, the new music innovations from America had arrived. Gramophone records were here. The early crystal radio receivers were commencing. New popular music such as Jazz and the American music was played. Dancing was stimulated by the new rhythms. Increasingly the Palace Cafe and Lounge area were promoting these Twenties innovations. On 29 December 1920 the Cafe was billed as the largest dance floor in Newark. One enterprising advertiser in the *Newark Herald* on 5th March 1921 said just below the Palace advertisement:-

> "Have a dance at home, All the latest Dance music on Zono Colombia and Regal Records can be obtained at Coynes Gramophone shop 48 Cartergate Newark. We repair Gramophones."

The Lounge area was also offered for club and committee meetings.

However the raison d'etre of the Palace was cinema. From the opening features the theatre began a cautious presentation of films for 48 years. The immense numbers of titles engaged cannot be recorded. However the highlights, trends and personnel will give a good idea throughout the years. The Great War 1914-18 had stultified the European film production. The American film studios had advanced hugely while still at peace. This huge advantage was never lost and today most films are American or are made with American money. However wherever possible the Palace sought the best films giving British films ample showings. The star system was commencing. Though the opening film 'King Solomons Mines' did not feature any names in the cast the trend was coming when a film would be sold largely on the names of the leading players. The first artist to achieve her name in enlarged print above the title was NAZIMOVA. Modestly described as the world's greatest actress and the star of 1,000 moods! Nazimova starred in 'An Eye for an Eye' a film showing an amazing blend of emotions ranging from the grotesque to the terrible. Other names in the first few months included Mabel Normand (in 'The Pest' and 'When Doctors Disagree'),

H. B. Warner ('The Man who turned White') and Francis X Bushman ('Romeo & Juliet').

At this time performances were continuous with full matinees. Prices of admission were billed as Balcony 1/8d + Tax 4d. = 2/-. Tickets in advance for balcony only 3d extra. Saloon 1/- + 3d Tax = 1/3d. Pit 7d + Tax 2d = 9d. Box office open 10 a.m. - 12 and 2 p.m. to 4 p.m. Children under 12 years of age - Mondays, Wednesdays and Fridays also matinees: Balcony 9d + Tax 3d = 1/-. Saloon 7d + Tax 2d = 9d. Pit 4½d + Tax 1½d = 6d. As the average wage of the local artisans was about 40 shillings a week a stratified audience was evident.

The complete Musical Programme for each change of film, which at first was every 3 days, was advertised on the front page adverts and consisted of at least 12 mainly classical pieces.

First indications of the immense popularity of the new cinema were made by the *Advertiser* 4th August 1920 which commented that 'there were record attendances at each and every performance'.

Of the great films D. W. Griffiths 'Broken Blossoms' came in late September, the length of which meant that there was not time for the orchestral concert.

The final week in 1920 the main feature was 'The Prince of Wales 50,000 Miles Tour'. The press report (*N.H.* 1/1/21) began

"Newark audiences are notoriously undemonstrative. However the large audience applauded loudly and long. It is a sufficient criterion that the film is super-excellent."

The hour long film ran 3 days.

The second features were mainly 2 reel 'scream' comedies, Charlie Chaplin, Mack Sennett and Mutt & Jeff. However, entrants to a children's beauty competition were introduced 4 per week. A weekly serial was introduced called Our Navy: a study of the British Navy. Part 10 was 'With the Grand Fleet in harbour'.

The theatre continued to try new things. The first live performance was not however initiated by the Palace management. When St Dunstans approached the Palace for a venue for a Blind Musicians Concert a Thursday afternoon matinee was allocated free of charge, on 3rd November 1920. The *Advertiser* report said of the light classicial concert that "a delightful atmosphere of music, only saddened by the unhappy affliction of the blinded artists, pervaded". The Palace Orchestra 'submitted a capital selection of music throughout the intermission'. The concert realised the sum of £83. On the heels of this concert came 'an enormous attraction'. A special engagement of Miss Marion Searle (Soprano) and Miss Margery Smith (Contralto) of "Madam Wilson Mould's Refined Entertainers and of Provincial Concerts", in their songs and duets. The performance each evening was between 7.30 and 8.30 p.m. prompt from 15th November 1920 for the week. The entertainment was completed by the usual films and serials.

The following week a definite shift was made from the classical to the 'popular'. The 'stupendous' programme was headed by Mr Harry Shipman the 'Rum' comedian supported by Miss Fanny Pinder (Soprano) also of "Madame Wilson Mould's Refined Entertainers". A colleague of Yorick's was quite outspoken: 'Judging from the applause which greeted the 'turns' at the Palace Monday, it is clearly evident that the management have taken a step in the right direction. There has also been a departure from the staid straight singing of last week '(lauded by Yorick)' and a 'rum' comedian was featured in the bill. Harry Shipman is indeed very rum and soon gets his audience in good 'spirits'. The audience took a little warming up, but it was soon evident that the lighter side was appeciated.'

On the music front

"Improvement follows improvement at the Palace, and good as the music side has been the orchestra has been replaced by a new talented London combination. The new musicians opened last evening and their initial success augers well for the future."

As will be seen in the next few months this was only the start in a series of changes in the search for music to appeal to the maximum audience. Another problem was to reach those discontents that boycotted the theatre from the day the Chauntry was gutted. In an article on Current Cinema Chit Chat by "Quiz" (supporter of rum comedians)

"The Old Chauntry was pulled down and the Palace grew on its ashes. Newark was provided with a beautiful theatre but unfortunately many people in the town have failed to realise the value of this modern building. Perhaps some Newarkers minds have been cramped and their vision narrowed. But they should wake to the fact that a luxurious building has been bequeathed to them by those who took the plunge and financed its erection. There should be a larger expression of gratitude."

Those discerning people that supported the retention of the Chauntry were precisely the type of people that would appreciate the top of the market stance adopted by the Palace. Not only was there a top quality restaurant, beautiful surroundings, exquisite music, films shown from the London cinemas, intelligent films made from stage plays and famous books but also the experimentation with live entertainment had given the Palace management the impetus to move towards a high class regional theatre. Christmas day was celebrated with a Christmas tree and an orchestra.

2. Professional Touring Theatre

On 22nd January 1921 the Palace advertised that next week Ralland and Cameron present by arrangement with MacDonald & Young 'Peg O' My Heart' a delightful comedy (not a film) by a first class London Company for six nights and Saturday matinee. Prices as usual. With 1,000 seats to sell at bargain prices it was a great gamble. Balcony seats only could be reserved. The Box Office opened from 10 a.m. to 10 p.m.

'Peg O' My Heart' was a 'comedy of youth' by J. Hartley Manners. Doors opened at 6 p.m. Also on the bill were special films shown from 6.15 to 7.15 when the play begins.

"The story concerns the aristocratic Chichester family. Peg is the daughter of an imperious Irishman and a lady of the Chichester family disinherited on her marriage to the Irishman. Her uncle Anthony had directed that Peg was to be educated and inherit £5,000 annually when her education had moulded her according to family traditions. Miss Heather Cooper as Peg arrives with a dirty looking mongrel under one arm and a big hand box under the other. This production took London by storm at the Globe and Comedy Theatre". On 29th January "seats are rapidly being booked up. Refreshments can be obtained in the Theatre or Cafe between Acts."

An ecstatic report reveals how Peg fared:

"Those critics who predicted that the Palace Theatre could never be filled a whole week even if plays were produced, have had their prophesy falsified. At the very first venture to bring a high class company to Newark the spacious theatre has been crowded each night this week with enthusiastic audiences who have been delighted with Peg of my Heart. In fact so eager have Newarkers been to patronise the efforts of the management to bring good class companies to Newark that those who did not go before 6.30 p.m. were met with the notice 'standing room only'. It is evident Newarkers will patronise a good class play and we understand others are booked for the near future."

The following week advertised a film of Sir Ernest Shackleton's Antarctic Expedition. In large letters on the advertisement it said 'Watch our adverts for next week' and announced a special Jazz Tea in the Cafe with afternoon orchestra.

Everyone watching out for the next weeks advert would see that Edwin T. Hayes principal company were to perform 'Hindle Wakes' at the Palace for a week commencing 14th February 1921, after playing at the Duke of York's theatre London for four years. In the cast was a very young Nan Marriott Watson who became well known in 'granny roles' on Film and Television in the fifties and sixties. Admission Prices were still held at Cinema levels.

This famous Lancashire play did not draw audiences as great as characterised the visit of Peg, "the houses during the week have been most gratifying and those who have witnessed the production have been loud in their praises."

At this time the Picturedrome was pulling all stops out to compete with both the Kinema and the Palace. The presentation of a successful Pantomime 'Little Red Riding Hood' late in January, a film starring Georges Carpentier the hero-worshipped boxer and other productions, were thorns in the side of Newark Cinemas Ltd. The outcome was that the Picturedrome was acquired by Newark Cinemas in April 1921 and closed soon after.

More monies were ploughed into the making of films which were getting longer, "Broken Blossoms", a D. W. Griffiths masterpiece had taken time from the normally scheduled orchestral concert. The Samuel Goldwyn film masterpiece endowed with "a power and poignancy never before equalled in a picture drama" titled 'Earth Bound' left only 20 minutes for other items when it commenced on 7th March 1921. In the same issue the Palace had 2 further separate adverts. The Palace Cafe was to hold "a special Jazz Tea on Thursday 10th March from 4 p.m. to 5.30 p.m. Tea & Dance ticket 1/6d reserved tables 2/-. Luncheons & Suppers. Special menu on Wednesdays and Saturdays. The Menu was: Soup, Fish, Cold Roast Beef, Ham, Tongue and Salads Vegetables." The other advert was to experiment with a full Dance Friday evening at 8.30 p.m. with the Castle orchestra. The cost 5/- each (including supper), "Apply Booking Office."

On 14th March A. Mainwaring Dunstan presented the actor manager Frank Forbes Robertson and his company in two plays for the week, "The Passing of the Third Floor Back" by Jerome K. Jerome and "Mice and Men" a romantic old world comedy by Madeleine Duchette Ryley. In this London company was Sir Donald Wolfit's highly regarded friend Frank Milray. Although no increase in admission prices was made a new category of seating was designated. Henceforth the "Dress Circle" was to be 3/- Reserved and Booked while the further back Circle seats remained at 2/- booked 3p extra. Mr Forbes Robertson had recently played opposite Martin Harvey in his uncle's (Sir Johnston Forbes Robertson) play "Pelleas and Melisande".

"Mice and Men" opens with Mark Embury the middle-aged philospher, once crossed in love, decides that it is his duty to marry and beget an heir. For this purpose he selects from the foundling hospital some healthy and very young girl. Now as is customary in the theatre the rest of the plot will only be revealed to those buying tickets!

> "The quality of the company can be judged by the fact that on April 17th last at the Theatre Royal Windsor the Company had the honour of performing before Princess Mary, the Princess Alice, the Prince Henry, the Prince George and the Earl of Athlone."

The plays were popular.

> "At the fall of the curtain, from a large and enthusiastic audience, the applause was so prolonged that Mr Frank Forbes Robertson was compelled to make a speech thanking the audience. Owing to the success of the play the Saturday matinee will change from "The Passing of the Third Floor Back" to "Mice and Men".

The next week 21st March J. Bannister Howard presented, for 3 days, the world famous laughter maker 'The Private Secretary' by Charles Hawtrey. From the Apollo, Savoy and the Aldwych Theatres London. This farce was over 40 years old and the reverend Robert Spalding was originally played by Sir Herbert Tree. The rest of the week showed Nazimova in her greatest production "The Brat", while Good Friday showed "The Woman" in a 7 part photoplay (the popular name used when a play was filmed). The advertisement concluded with a new regulation 'Babies in arms not admitted to any performance'!

Easter holiday week provided, twice nightly, a Grand Holiday Programme of Varieties & Pictures. 'A special engagement at enormous cost the world celebrated A. D. Robbins The Canadian Cycle Tamer' supported by Kingsford and Paff (comedy musical speciality) and Mabel

Roma original and artistic dancer, plus films. This was more Kinema and Picturedrome fare. Prices were identical to Cinema charges.

On Warrior's Day, Thursday, 31st March, a special matinee was held in aid of Earl Haig's fund for relief of ex servicemen in distress. Miss U. Kentish-Wright's Amateur Company presented under the patronage of the Mayor & Mayoress of Newark the brilliant play 'His Excellency the Governor' by kind permission of the Directors of the Palace Theatre. Prices were high, the dress circle costing 4/- and the Pit 1/-. However it was the tradition of charities to contribute generously to splendid causes. The Palace Orchestra rendered musical selections from 2.30 - 3 p.m. and during the intervals.

The innovative Bank Holiday programme of variety and films brought large audiences who were appreciative of Mr A D. Robbins The Canadian Cycle Tamer. 'His performance is one long scream particularly when members of the audience are invited to ride his bronco bicycle'.

3.   Charles Doran and Shakespeare

Some readers may have wondered who was the Donald Wolfit that I have quoted earlier in The Palace Years. Born in 1902 in London Road, Balderton, Donald had a burning ambition from his early years to become an actor. Although discouraged by his respectable middle class family, because of its reputation and uncertainties, he persisted. After amateur experience at the Robin Hood Theatre, Averham, he soon graduated to the professional stage. After a long and distinguished career in the unfashionable theatre he was Knighted for his services in 1957. Sir Donald Wolfit died still at the peak of his career in 1968.

His first professional engagement was the Charles Doran Shakespearean Company.

> "In the Spring I was sent for and asked by Mr Doran if the newly built theatre in my own home town was a suitable date to play. I said it was, and within six months of the commencement of my professional career I found myself facing a Newark audience as Lancelot Gobbo in 'The Merchant of Venice', Trinculo in 'The Tempest', a witch in 'Macbeth' and Second Gravedigger in 'Hamlet' and acquitting myself creditably."

"The Charles Doran company presented for the week commencing 5th April 1921 8 performances, 2 performances of 'The Merchant of Venice', one each of 'Hamlet', 'As You Like It', 'Taming of the Shrew',

*Touring Actor Manager Charles Doran as Hamlet. He gave Donald Wolfit
his first job in the theatre.*

PALACE THEATRE,

APPLETONGATE, NEWARK.

Licensed for Stage Plays, Music, Singing and Dancing, and Cinematograph Exhibitions.

Proprietors ... ... **NEWARK CINEMAS, Ltd.**
Manager ... ... **J. W. ARMSTRONG.**

TUESDAY, APRIL 5th, 1921.

7-15 ONCE NIGHTLY 7-15
DOORS OPEN 6-30. EARLY DOORS 6 O'CLOCK.

Mr. CHARLES DORAN & his Shakespearean Company.

SHAKESPEARE'S TRAGEDY:

HAMLET

Claudius, King of Denmark	REGINALD JARMAN
Hamlet, Son of the late and Nephew to the present King	CHARLES DORAN
Horatio, Friend to Hamlet	ERIC ADENEY
Polonius, Lord Chamberlain	EDWARD J. WOOD
Laertes, his Son	ALEXANDER BROWNLOW
Rosencrantz	ROBERT LANG
Guildenstern } Courtiers {	W. J. CULFF
Osric	FRANK HENDON
A Priest	WILLIAM DUKE
Marcellus } Officers {	R. NEIL PORTER
Bernardo	TERRANCE MILLBROOK
Francisco, a Soldier	HENRY ROSTROM
Ghost of Hamlet's Father	ARTHUR YOUNG
First Player	HILTON EDWARDS
Second Player	T. RICHARDS
Player Queen	NOELLE SONNING
First Gravedigger	R. TUDOR OWEN
Second Gravedigger	DONALD WOOLFITT
Gertrude, Queen of Denmark	EDITH SHARP
Ophelia, Daughter to Polonius	MURIEL HUTCHINSON

Lords, Ladies, Attendants.

Scene: ELSINORE.

ACT 1—Scene 1	Elsinore. Platform before the Castle	ACT 2—Scene 1		A Corridor of the Castle
Scene 2	The Hall of the Castle	Scene 2		The Queen's Apartments
Scene 3	The Platform	Scene 3		A Corridor of the Castle
Scene 4	A more remote part	Scene 4		The Hall of the Castle
Scene 5	The Hall of the Castle		Interval of 8 Minutes	
Scene 6	The Same — a few hours later	ACT 3—Scene 1		A Churchyard
	Interval of 8 Minutes.	Scene 2		A Corridor
		Scene 3		A Hall of the Castle

The Curtain will be lowered after Scene 1, Act 1, to denote the passing of time.

The Play produced by CHARLES DORAN.

Stage Manager		ALEXANDER BROWNLOW
	For	ERIC ADENEY
Assistant Stage Manager	Mr. CHARLES	DONALD WOOLFITT
	DORAN	HILTON EDWARDS
Advance Manager		WALTER DEAN
Business Manager		CHARLES LAKE

During the Evening the Orchestra will perform from the following Selections of Music.

Musical Director:

March	"Sons of the Brave"	T. Bidgood
Suite	"Old Kensington"	L. Sturdy
Georgian Dance	"Mistress Penelope"	W. Arnold
Selection	"Merrie England"	E. German
Serenade		Leoncavallo
Pas Seul	"Pirouette"	H. Finck
Three Dances	"Nell Gwyn"	E. German

SPECIAL MATINEE ON SATURDAY AT 2-30 P.M.

Seats can be Booked at Palace Box Office, 10-30 a.m. to 10 p.m.

SEATS BOOKED BY TELEPHONE must be claimed
10 minutes before rise of Curtain or will be sold. **'Phone 199.**

NO MONEY RETURNED. CHILDREN IN ARMS NOT ADMITTED.

The Management reserve the right to refuse admission

REFRESHMENTS can be obtained in the Theatre or Cafe between Acts or during the Performance.

Playbill for Hamlet with Donald Wolfit as second gravedigger and assistant Stage Manager.

'The Tempest', 'Julius Caesar' and the Scottish play!

'Mr Doran is in the fore rank of Shakespearean players. He was in former days with Sir Herbert Tree and H. B. Irving. It is hoped that the support will be such as to warrant the Shakespeare week becoming an annual fixture.'

Touring as Actor Manager was a relatively new departure for Charles Doran. The week went well. Lovers of the immortal bard loudly chanting the praises of Mr Charles Doran and his talented company, commending the Palace management and the general manager Mr Armstrong on their enterprise in securing for Newark audiences such a first rate of gathering of artists giving sterling expositions of the Shakespeare tragedies-comedies. One could have wished that this first essay to bring before Newarkers high dramatic art had been more generously seconded by the public.

'The Palace should have been placed in the position of having to announce House Full at every performance. But unfortunately this has not been so, a circumstance which can be attributed to the trade depression.'

The company had a magnificent reception from the audiences each night. The applause loud and sustained. Mr Doran had to concede a speech each evening. He acknowledged the promise of Mr Woolfitt

'who had allowed him to play Shylock. However if they (the Company) did not do well at Newark he (Mr Woolfitt) would be hanged in the next town.'

"Mr Woolfitt" was not always so popular with Mr Doran. In the first play he appeared with Doran as Brutus in Julius Ceaser. He was one of 3 members of the Company who had to carry the dead Brutus away. As he hoisted the defunct tragedian up on his shoulders the corpse in a far from Roman voice hissed 'for Gods sake mind my toupee'. Today such a mammoth schedule of 7 different plays in a weeks visit would be unthinkable and cost a fortune.

It would of course have been very difficult to fill the 1,300 seat theatre. Performing 7 different plays in a week the minimum cost to see every play in the pit would have been 63d equivalent to an artisan's entire wage for a week and a half.

However the final performances were euphoric. Charles Doran thanked everyone including the Conductress and the orchestra who had not only played the incidental music during the performance but played a selection of classical music through the interval and also for her little personal kindnesses.

The Palace produced a leaflet programme which advertised forthcom-

George Burnley - Musical Director for the Palace.

ing Varieties, Plays and Pictures. The programme cost 2d. The next week was headed by the film 'Kismet' supported by Mr Karl Edwards (popular comedian) assisted by Rosie Devere. They presented a laughable original musical comedy sketch entitled 'Explanations'. Jack Patterson an original eccentric juggler completed the bill. As the competition with the Picturedrome was coming to a head these Cinema and 'Turns' programmes which the Picturedrome specialized in must have reduced the patronage of the independent cinema especially as the Kinema sister theatre to the Palace also continued presenting similar fare. The comedy sketch was probably a taster for the musical comedies that were to come.

Commencing on 25th April for a week was the powerful play 'A Royal Divorce' by W. G. Wills. This historical drama was set at the time of the battle of Waterloo and concerned the politics and relationships within the court of Napoleon Bonaparte. Written in 1891 this great play now in its 30th year of touring has been seen by many millions of playgoers. The leading players were Ronald Bayne, Agnes Verity and a young Wilfred Lawson in a minor role.

This was followed on 2nd May 1921 for a week by the Musical Comedy 'Betty' supplied by MacDonald & Young. Written by Frederick Lonsdale & Gladys Unger. Music by Paul Rubens. So impressed were the Palace Management that George Burnley the Musical Director of 'Betty' was employed to fill the elusive position of Musical Director of the Palace. He remained there for over ten years.

The press were delighted

"Mr Armstrong, the Palace manager, in the series of stage plays he has secured for Newark patrons, has been fortunate in booking the finest on each occasion and his latest acquisition this week 'Betty' is among the best of the bunch. Notwithstanding the trade depression and consequent lack of ready money there have been satisfactory audiences and the adventures of the coy and winsome kitchen maid Betty have been enthusiastically followed and applauded. There should be crowded houses at both performances today (Saturday). This presentation ended the season and cinema returned."

On Friday 20th at 8 p.m. sharp Mr Charles E. Best gave an Exposition of the Kelham Oilfields titled 'A History of Mineral Developments in the Newark District'. Special films will be shown illustrating the Oil Industry. Admission by invitation ticket only. The Newark Herald took 4 columns reporting the meeting. For the summer prices for cinema only were reduced and became:-

	Balcony	Saloon	Pit
Were	2/-d	1/6d	1/3d
Summer	1/6d	1/3d	9d

Live entertainment soon returned. On 11th July for 3 nights Miss Mona Glyn introduced us to the great success from the Royalty Theatre 'Billeted'. A comedy by F. Tennyson. The play was preceded by the supreme Nazimova in her best picture "Madame Peacock".

This was followed, for 3 days 4th to 6th August, with 'Lord Richard in The Pantry' adapted from Martin Swaynes novel, from the Criterion Theatre London, with Lillie Soutter as Cook and Richard Cooper as Lord Richard.

A return to Musical Comedy came in 'Girl in the Taxi' direct from the Lyric Theatre by Frederick Fenn & Arthur Wimperis (from the French). Music by Jean Gilbert. On 15th August for 3 nights.

On 22nd August for 3 nights Ventom Swifts record success 'All Aboard'. 1921 version, book & lyrics by Bert H. Delmar. A song show revue, Original Comedy, Novelty Dancing. In fact almost a variety show but with a theme.

4. Stage Shows - a Regular Feature

The live shows were now a regular feature. Truly Newark had a theatre.

On 29th August for 6 nights J. Bannister Howard's chief company came in the merriest, brightest, and greatest of all musical comedies 'The Belle of New York'.

The next presentation on 12th September 1921 for 3 nights was Leslie Kyle in the great success from the Garrick Theatre the much discussed farce 'The Girl from Ciro's' adapted from the French by Pierre Verber.

On 26th September for 6 nights billed as the musical event of the Season was Macdonald & Young's 'The Maid of the Mountains'. Book by Frederick Lonsdale. Reginald Purdell was in the cast. Confident of success the 'Free List' was entirely suspended.

This was followed by 3 days of Wyn Weaver's London Company in "the funniest farce of the century". 'Fair and Warmer', from the Prince of Wales Theatre London, where it played to crowded houses for over

500 performances. This played to packed houses.

On October 10th for 3 nights came J. Bannister Howard's company in Wilson Barrett's great success 'The Silver King' a melodrama of redemption.

On Thursday afternoon 13th October a further high class charity concert was organised in aid of St Dunstans Hostel for the blind. Ticket prices beween 4/- and 1/3d were above theatre prices but Newarkers always supported a good cause.

The regular live theatre continued with the most beautiful of all modern love stories 'The Blue Lagoon' founded on H. DeVere Stacpoole's world-famous novel. The production by J. Bannister Howard was

"as played to record houses at the Prince of Wales Theatre London."

The story will be familiar to cinema viewers having been filmed in 1948 with Jean Simmons and relatively recently with Brooke Shields. The young castaway lovers were played on stage by Nan Marriott Watson (her second visit to Newark) and Ronald Buchanan.

The remarkable weekly live theatre of high quality continued through October, into mid December. On 24th October the musical play 'Tonights the Night' (based on "The Pink Dominoes") came for 3 nights. Book by Frederick Thompson. Music by Paul Rubens with Roddy Hughes a later film star. 31st October for 3 days Cecil Barth's Company in Brandon Thomas's famous farcical comedy 'Charley's Aunt'. This was followed by the 4 act comedy 'Paddy The Next Best Thing' by Mackay & Ord. Lady (Arthur) Lever wrote 'Brown Sugar' a light comedy which came for 3 nights. This was followed by Easton Pickering in 'The Very Idea' a farce by William le Baron from St. Martin's Theatre London. This was stated as "for adults only" in which our hero thwarts a eugenic scheme to provide him with an heir.

On Sunday evening 27th November 1921 a high class concert was arranged 'For The Children's Sake' organisation. It was in aid of the fund to provide the poor children of Newark with a new year treat organised by the Newark Tradesmens Association. Members of Madame Wilson-Mould's famous Nottingham concert party with an elocutionist Mrs Harold Ledger from the south of England with musical selections by the augmented orchestra of the Palace Theatre under the baton of George Burnley. Tickets were priced at cinema level. This type of entertainment was considered acceptable on a Sunday when so much public entertainment would not be countenanced. Surprisingly Xmas day was always open for Theatre business unless of course Xmas Day was also a Sunday.

Live entertainment continued with the New Whirligig Revue. This was followed by a large production lasting 6 nights . This Great Musical Super Revue 'Hullo America 1921'. It starred Peggy O'Dare, Philip H. Ellis, Jack Goodson and Gordon Courtney. However on the Monday and Tuesday evenings the cast was without 2 of the principals which was not popular.

Finally Ernest E Norris, the well known character actor starred in 'The Walls of Jericho' by Arthur Sutro billed as the play of the century. Perhaps being just before Xmas business was not good.

The new year season of live entertainment began on 2nd January 1922. Mr Charles Stewart presented for the first time in Newark the brilliant comedy from the Criterion London 'A Pair Of Silk Stockings' by Cyril Harcourt. This was followed by the Palace's first Pantomime "Cinderella". This was probably brought about by the success of the Picturedrome's pantomime in January 1921. It was held for a full week with matinees.

'The Arcadians' came for 3 days on 16th January. It was billed as 'the prettiest and best musical comedy not only at this moment but which our stage has seen for years'. (*Daily Mail*)

It will be noticed that the three day presentations began on a Monday thus giving the company the dark Sunday to organise the stage. Following 'The Arcadians' on Thursday and Saturday afternoon was a Grand Pageant called 'Children Through the Centuries' with over 200 performers. Under distinguished patronage in aid of the waifs and strays.

Week commencing 23rd January Mr Arthur Gibbons Company, making their first visit to Newark, present the enormously successful comedy 'The Rotters' from London's West End theatres.

The following week Macdonald and Young presented 'Nothing But The Truth' a comedy starring Allan Dale and Eileen Lovett Janison written by James Montgomery. 'When Knights Were Bold' by Charles Harlow followed. It claimed the longest run of the century. The silent film 'Daddy Longlegs' was transferred to the stage by Macdonald & Young. It starred Miss Olga Lindo and Harry C. Robinson.

From mid February until the end of the month live shows both professional and amateur filled the Palace stage. On the 20th for 3 days came 'The Weekend' by W. W. Ellis. The actual London Company brought Mademoiselle Marguerite Pordes as Lucille as presented at the Kingsway Theatre. It was a resounding success. Thursday 23rd a matinee of the New Comedy 'Clipped Wings' was presented in aid of the London Association for the Blind, written by Mrs K. M. Garner the local authoress who previously wrote the sketches in the dramatic entertainment at the Palace on 11th January 1921. Katherine Garner was a prolific local writer who was accustomed to producing sketches plays and entertainments for charitable causes during and after the Great War. One of her wartime entertainments, part song, part parody and part fantasy - entitled 'The intervention of Santa Claus' included the boy Woolfitt who played 'a gentleman styled Herr Buffen-Gruffen (not a bad sort of German)'. The idea of a boy playing a German seemed the only acceptable way of obtaining someone to play a member of the hated German race. With great difficulty Mr Garner approached Woolfitt's father who very reluctantly gave his consent after 'great pressure' from Mr Garner on the understanding that rehearsals must not interfere with his school homework. The enraptured Woolfitt had started the long journey to a knighthood. Even though suffering acute stage fright he was still observant of all around him.

> "I shall always remember the officer who could not learn the verses of a parody and wrote them out in large print onto cards which he placed between the footlights so that he could stoop down and read them during the 'tum-ti-tum-tum' between verses."

On Saturday 25th February the women's Unionist and Conservative Association presented an entertainment at the Palace Theatre with songs, fancy dances, short sketches, etc. The month ended with the professional comedy 'The Cinderella Man' by Edward Childs Carpenter starring Miss Sarah Benedict from the Queens Theatre London.

March 1922 was just as crowded. Miss Mary Byron and her London Company came in 'French Leave' by Reginald Berkeley. Film of the wedding of Princess Mary to the Prince of Wales preceded the presentation of the world famous comic opera 'The Chocolate Soldier'. This was followed by 'The Naughty Wife' a comedy by Fred Jackson. At the end of the month a special film in colour was shown called 'Poor Butterfly' along with film of the Lincoln handicap race.

April opened with the mighty religious play 'Sign of The Cross' by

William Barrett for the week. The William McLaren company with Mr McLaren starring as the unlikely named Roman Prefect Marcus Superbus Patrons were advised to book early. The popular musical comedy "The Quaker Girl" arrived for 3 days attracting large audiences.

After a brief lull in live presentations came 'Betty at Bay' a comedy by Jessie Porter for 6 days. The play was preceded by film of the English Cup Final (the disputed goal) and orchestral items.

The next live shows came on 22nd May 1922 for 3 days. Arthur Bourchier's Company came in 'At the Villa Rose' by A. E. W. Mason, direct from the Strand Theatre with the full London cast.

The cafe advert 'Have you tried our freshly frozen ice cream' was ominous for the production. The press wrote 'Hot weather was not conducive to a large theatre audience.' It seems that the Newark summer dip in audiences was always with us. The previous summer cinema prices had been reduced. However the right shows would always sell.

June commenced with a week of Grand Opera from the celebrated John Ridding Grand Opera Company for a week with a different presentation every evening, Il Trovatore, Rigoletto, Faust, La Traviata, Maritiana and The Bohemian Girl. The only other June production was Fred le Cren's 'The Belle of Madrid' a musical farcial extravaganza.

July was devoted entirely to films. Ballet first featured at the Palace on celluloid with Anna Pavlova and the Russian Ballet supported by Princess Mary's Wedding presents. From 31st July to 2nd August 1922 a full Variety programme was presented. Top of the Bill was Cicely Courtneidge. The famous Vaudeville star assisted by Peter Holden. The full variety programme was composed of Mollie O'Moore (vocalist), La coupe (all British dance), Dan Polyat, Bernard (and a pack of cards) and Vivien Foster 'the vicar of mirth' catchphrase 'Yes I think so', one of the first performers popularised by the new Radio age. Live theatre continued in August with return visits of 'Maid of the Mountains', with Vera McDonald and Helen Beal and 'The Quaker Girl'.

The autumn season began 4th September with Cusick & Eccles presentation of 'Tickled to Death' 'the Lancashire musical comedy revue' starring Ernie King, Ethel Colyer, 4 Dancing Daises and Arthur Ronald (phenomenal soprano).

A large advertisement was given for the cafe to remind patrons of its delights and attract visitors from the surrounding areas.

Cicely Courtneidge

"Get out of the Rut'. To country visitors to Newark. 'Why put up with inconveniences when you can obtain the following comforts and advantages at the 'PALACE THEATRE CAFE'. Accomodation for motors. Lock up for Motor cycles and cycles. Free wash and brush up. Free cloakroom and parcel office. Public Telephone. Writing room. High class refreshments. Luncheons, Teas, Suppers. The Palace Cafe has been rightly termed - A Home from Home."

Live entertainment continued with the Macey and Marcelle production of 'The Maid of the South' a musical comedy by John Ware in 3 scenes starring Bert Morland, Robert Gilmour and including 'a Beauty Chorus'.

5.   More Shakespeare and Future Stars

In complete contrast came the much awaited return of the Charles Doran Shakespeare Company 18th to 24th September. Donald Woolfitt had moved on but the Company contained a wealth of actors who were destined to be famous. The leading lady was Miss Barbara Everest, "the charming Shakespearean actress, who is returning to the legitimate stage after a successful season in film work." Further down the cast were: Ralph Richardson, later to be knighted, Cecil Parker, a giant in British films, that obese villain Frances L. Sullivan, Norman Shelley one of the truly great radio voices as well as stage and film actor, and finally Abraham Sofaer whose deep sepulcheral voice was instantly distinguishable equally on stage, film and especially radio. Who would not have wished to see a cast with such presence and talent?

The programme of six evenings and two matinees comprised Monday 'Taming of the Shrew', Tuesday 'The Merchant of Venice', Wednesday 'A Midsummer Nights Dream', Thursday 'Macbeth', Friday 'Twelfth Night', Saturday 'Hamlet' and the matinees 'Julius Caesar' and 'A Midsummer Nights Dream'.

Finishing September was the musical comedy 'Sunny Spain'. Beginning this week also was a series of teatime dances every afternoon except Fridays from 4 p.m. to 5.30 p.m in the Cafe Ballroom. The admission price including tea was one shilling. (5p) The Palace orchestra were in attendance with all the latest music. No doubt George Burnley provided a first class programme. An evening Dance was also tried from 7.30 to 10 p.m. also 1/-.

October presented 'Peg O My Heart' and 'Betty' both repeats followed by Franz Lehar's 'The Merry Widow'. Finishing October was Gwyneth Keys in 'Polly with a Past', a farce, who, after the conclusion of the play gave a selection from her repertoire of character studies. November began with 'The Bill of Divorcement' which was preceded by a one act play called 'Daylight Saving'. On Sunday 5th November a Grand Concert was given in aid of The Newark Branch of NUR Orphans appeal. The Retford Choral union of 75 voices entertained the audience. On the 6th November came the play 'Edge Of Beyond' adapted from the novel by Gertrude Page. On 13th November came Payne Seddon's production of 'Eliza Comes to Stay' from the Criterian Theatre London a 3 act farce by H. V. Esmond.

On Friday 10th October the Palace became host to a mass Political meeting held by the Marquis of Titchfield, the conservative candidate at the forthcoming election. *The Advertiser* gave five columns which filled one page of the paper. The Earl of Ancaster in his speech exposed Nationalisation and the Capital Levy. Mr David Gilmour trade unionist leader declared that the Socialist Labour Party are 'friends of every country but their own'. Other gems included 'Every vote not given for Lord Titchfield is a vote for socialism and real ruin'. 'Ex servicemen vote for Lord Titchfield and make your pensions safe and secure'.

I regret that I am unable to find any balancing speeches from other parties that were no doubt as passionate in denouncing the opposition. A return to normal fare came with 'Over The Hill' modestly described as 'the worlds greatest film'. A tale of a mother's love and a child's forgetfulness. Live entertainment for late November and early December was a musical comedy called 'Chiffon Dear' followed by 'Little Biddy O'Farrell'.

On the 9th December the Newark division of the Women's Conservative Association presented a Grand Matinee with a children's ballet, solo dances, plays and musical items. The Patron was The Marquis of Titchfield. The admission price was 3/-.

A Grand Orchestral and Choral Concert had been held on 3rd December under the direction of Mr George Burnley. It was planned for further Sunday concerts to be given. However the report stated that 'there should have been more listeners to the music'. A splendid programme quite in keeping with the Sabbath evening.

December finished with the Italian film masterpiece 'Cabiria', Gabriele D'Annunzio's classic of the Roman Empire. This was followed by Victor Sardons' 'Theodora' with a cast of over 25,000 performers. These show the extent of progress in silent films. In this era the language barrier of talkies hadn't come. All films had subtitles which made it easier for audiences to accept foreign films.

6.   Newark Cinemas Ltd. Early Finances

After fifteen months of trading by Newark Cinemas Ltd., the financial position was assessed and the financial results given for the period ending 31st December 1921 at the annual general meeting 16th February 1922. The only figures given are the net profit for the period after tax and the subsequent allocation of the £2,155 profit to shareholders in the form of dividends and the balance carried forward. The amount allocated of a 5% dividend is £1925. This immediately shows that the capital of the company fell far short of the £55,000 subscription shares mentioned in the 1920 Prospectus. The capital actually subscribed is about £38,000. A 5% dividend also looks well below the estimates given in the prospectus which stated that "if an average of only a third of the cinema's seats were filled, a 10% divided would be payable." With no other financial records available guesses have to be made. Firstly Newark Cinemas acquired The Picturedrome in April 1921 and did not dispose of the lease until November 1922. This cost would have had to be temporary absorbed.

Reviewing the past years work Mr Graham said that
" the directors had introduced films, varieties and plays at the Palace Theatre, and they had decided that of the three, plays were most appreciated by the Newark Public."

The best London shows had been booked for the coming season and he appealed to the Newark Public to support them in their efforts to maintain a first class programme. A vote of thanks was given to the Staffs of the Palace and the Kinema and especially the managers Mr J. Armstrong and Mr Cann and Miss Ralph the cafe manageress for the way in which they had looked after the interests of the Company.

The 1922 results were announced at the AGM 1st March 1923 at the Palace Theatre Cafe. The base figure of net profit was £1494 and a dividend of 3% was made. This again appeared disappointing. However the monies from the sale of the Picturedrome lease may not have been included. The lease was assigned to John H. Knight a Newark grocer on 23 November 1922.

In April 1922 the small 300 seater Cinema Beaumond Hall had been purchased. This would be a sizeable outlay and again confuses the financial situation. Once the lease had been acquired Beaumond Hall continued to show films leaving the Palace to concentrate upon live performances without rationing cinema devotees. However Beaumond Hall ceased to show films in April 1923 and became a Salvation Army Citadel in 1924.

Mr Graham in seconding the Balance sheet said that the Directors would endeavour to secure plays by the best companies but they must have more support from the Newark public. A vote of thanks was given to Mr Armstrong, Mr Cann, Miss Ralph and the Staff of the Palace for their untiring work during the past year and said that the highly satisfactory position of the company was to a large extent due to their capable management. The initial early years had been weathered and the remaining history of Newark Cinemas Ltd., is one long success until they astutely sold the company in 1952 at the dawn of television for £130,000 or £1.75 per share.

1923 commenced with the musical comedy 'Sally' followed by the pantomime 'Red Riding Hood' for six nights and three matinees containing 11 scenes and Les Classiques from the London Palladium admission varied from 3/- to 9d. On 1st February at 2.30 p.m. came a benefit for the Newark & District Nursing Association with the Bessie Unwin Grand Concert Party from Sheffield price 3/-. The musical comedy film 'The Bohemian Girl' followed, starring Gladys Cooper, C. Aubrey Smith, Ellen Terry and Ivor Novello, while live shows in February included, 'Clothes and the Woman', a light comedy and the massive production of 'Chu Chin Chow' for a full week with a cast of over 50. Frank Forbes Robertson returned with 'David Garrick' and 'Call of the Road'. This production was previewing in Newark before the London presentation. It was followed by 'The Widow's Husband'. Bessie Unwins Grand Concert Party returned for a sacred concert on Sunday 11th February. Prices were 1/3d and 9d.

In March plays continued with 'Thank You Phillips', and Cecile Barclay with Rupert Lister in 'The Great Adventurer'. The big film was

Gladys Cooper with Ellen Tery in the film "The Bohemian Girl".

'Atlantide' from the Pierre Benoit novel. This was followed in early April by the film 'Dont Tell Everything' "a real life picture to please the women, and give a few hints to the man"!

May was rich in stage productions. It began with 'Tons of Money' billed as London's greatest attraction recently performed before HM the King. This was followed by 'A Little Bit Of Fluff' and 'General Post'. Miss Viola Compton then came with the Nottingham Repertory Company in 'The School for Scandal'. The month ended with Reginald Nugent, Georgina Winter and Jane Welsh in 'The Way of an Eagle'.

June and July had a break in live theatre. The cinema had developed picture plays in which plays were filmed much like the stage play acted by talented British actors and actresses. The Kinema was ending live variety and concentrating solely on cinema.

The stage season began late August with Iris Hoey and Cyril Raymond in 'Jill the Giant Killer'. The Palace continued with some excellent films of London Plays 'The Taming of the Shrew' (Shakespeare) 'A Stage Romance' (life of Edmund Kean). The planned visit of the stage play 'Are You A Mason' was postponed owing to unavoidable circumstances! However the visit of Stella Patrick Campbell as Ann Carfax in Ethel M. Dell's novel 'The Knave of Diamonds' must have lessened the disappointment.

7.   Blockbuster Movies

A series of blockbuster films came in the autumn including Rudolph Valentino and Gloria Swanson in Elinor Glyn's novel 'Beyond the Rocks' and 'The Four Horsemen of the Apocalypse'. Patrons were assured that the film would be shown for the full two hour screening as seen at the Palace Theatre London. Billed as 'the masterpiece of the age' costing £250,000 with special effects and orchestra. The local paper said that in this scenario of recording mighty events, the screen's superiority over the stage was recognised by the critics after the first showings of "The Four Horsemen".

On the 26th October the Palace presented a Star Concert with Marie Hall (world renowned violinist), Stella Carol (the celebrated coloratura soprano) and Edward Brightwell (well known pianist of Queen's and Albert Halls London). Tickets were priced at 4/- Dress Circle, 3/-

Orchestra stalls, 2/6d Upper Circle, 1/6 Saloon. At the end of October the P. G. Wodehouse musical comedy play 'Kissing Time' occupied the stage. This was followed by a Pageant 'Children in Fiction' in aid of the Waif's and Strays Society on the 12th to 14th November produced by Mr & Mrs Ernest Randall. Prices 3/- to 1/3d. This was followed by D. W. Griffiths' great cinema masterpiece 'Orphans of the Storm' starring Lillian and Dorothy Gish as the two orphans. The film will be shown exactly as in London. The tremendous popularity of "The Four Horseman" was underlined by the advert continuing 'Hundreds were disappointed in not being able to obtain seats to see 'The Four Horsemen'. Make sure of securing a good seat by booking early. Seats can be reserved at 1/6d.

However the stage plays were yielding crowded houses. 'Kissing Time' with Miss Mary Rigby and Miss Florence Hunter and Mr Leo Franklyn, a comedian of exceptional ability, evoked much laughter. Despite the closure of Beaumond Hall in April Newark was enjoying the best of live and celluloid entertainment.

From 19th-21st November Frank Forbes Robertson returned for the third visit with new production 'Rosemary' and repeat presentations of 'Mice and Men' and 'Call of the Road'. With heavy bookings expected patrons were urged to secure their seats early. On the 30th November a piano recital was given by Mark Hambourg. Prices were high 5/9d, 3/6d, 2/4d and 1/6d.

On 13th December 'Sweet Lavender' the comedy by Pinero was staged by a company of Newark amateurs in aid of the blind. This was followed by Ida Stratham in the play 'Butterfly on the Wheel'. On Thursday 27th December the Nottingham Amateur Dramatic Club presented in aid of the Mayors Imperial War Relief Fund 'Mr Pim Passes By' the leading Christmas attraction. However audiences were not great. The local press felt that the amateur billing made the general public sceptical of their ability. Probably it was just the parochial feeling about amateurs from Nottingham? I would imagine that the special notice in the *Newark Advertiser* that turkeys, geese and hares will be given to patrons in lucky seats was perhaps not as welcome on 27th December especially in a world without freezers and fridges.

Live entertainments began on the last day of December 1923 until 5th January with Will Parkin's pantomime 'Aladdin and his Wonderful

Lamp'. This was followed by Lonsdale's musical 'Lady of the Rose' which enjoyed crowded houses and 'The Man from Toronto' a comedy by Douglas Murray.

The company of Newark Amateurs repeated Pinero's comedy 'Sweet Lavender' in aid of Newark and District Hospital appeal on 17th and 18th January. Prices of admission were from 4/-. There was also a three night visit of the Cooptimists (the A Company) from London. "A pierrotic entertainment."

In February the Farnborough Boys Band held a concert for the National Childrens Homes. International Golfer Tom Williamson was in the Chair. At the end of February an all British Film week was held with vocalists singing appropriate songs. On Sunday 9th March the Lincoln Old Comrades Military Band gave a concert. Malcolm Tearle starred in the play from Wyndhams Theatre 'Passers By'. An official film on the Battle of Jutland was introduced by lecturer Lieutenant A. E. Spry of the Royal Navy Volunteer Reserve.

In May the mammoth film 'If Winter Comes' appeared followed by the musical play 'Sybil', and 'Chu Chin Chow' was repeated with Betty Blythe and Herbert Langley. Alongside the professionals came a benefit for the Nursing Association by the Strolling Players an entertainment produced by another professional Mrs Lewis Ransome. Things quietened down through the early summer and in time for the late summer and autumn season the new billiard room was opened on the first floor of the Palace Theatre.

August provided two further D. W. Griffiths films; 'One Exciting Night' and 'Way Down East' both for a week with Lillian Gish and Richard Bartholeness. This was followed by Norma Talmadge in 'Enemies of Society' and 'The Great White Silence' an account of Scott's journey to the Antarctic.

It was at this time that good wireless transmission reached Newark. Films continued with 'One of the Blood' Douglas Fairbanks and Edna Purvience in Charles Chaplin's 'A Woman of Paris' both for the week.

Live entertainment returned on the 29th September when 'Charley's Aunt' paid a return visit. This was followed by the film in 5 reels of 'The British Empire Exhibition at Wembley' with no half prices on evening showings. At the end of October came the farcical musical comedy 'Toni' from the Shaftsbury theatre which played to packed houses. This was followed by a repeat showing of 'The Belle of New York'.

November introduced audiences to the play 'Bunty Pulls the Strings' which was followed by Mrs Lewis Ransome presenting the Newark Amateur Dramtic Society in 'Liberty Hall' a Saturday matinee and the following Monday, Tuesday and Wednesday in aid of the Newark Hospital and Nursing association. Prices were Monday 4/-, Tuesday and Wednesday 3/-.

In December the prices for admission were reduced to Circle 1/3, Saloon 9d and Pit 4d. This no doubt helped the poorer classes with unemployment at a high level. The Xmas day presentation for one day was the film 'The Beloved Vagabond'.

1925 opened with the pantomime 'The Babes in the Wood' 'A Stupendous attraction', another Percy H. Holmshaw production. Prices were 3/- Dress Circle, 2/- Upper Circle & Orchestra Stalls, 1/3 Saloon, 9d Pit. Special reduced prices for children on Monday and Friday evenings and the three matinees. This was followed by the musical comedy 'Irene' from London's Empire Theatre starring Harry Ray and Billee Dixon.

In February the Palace presented the famous O'Mara Opera Company. "The musical event of the season." "Grand Opera in English On Tour since 1912." Cyn Lais Gibbs the producer presented 4 operas in the three day engagement. Monday Verdi's 'Il Trovatore', Tuesday Bizet's 'Carmen', Wednesday matinee Verdi's 'Rigoletto and Wednesday evening Balfe's 'Bohemian Girl'.

The parade of high class live and cinema entertainment continued. On 8th March the Cresswell Colliery Prize Band gave 2 Grand Concerts with 'renowned' artist Master Joseph Farrington (juvenile cornet) Frank Webb (Euphonium) Alfred Rose (Baritone) and J. W. Bradshaw (violin). This was followed by the revue 'Laughing Time' and The Young Helpers League gave a variety concert in aid of the Dr Barnado's organisation. This was followed by the new musical farce direct from the Lyric Theatre London 'Whirled into Happiness'.

A variety of excellent films also arrived. The world's most perilous camera expedition 'Trailing African Wild Animals' a six reel entertainment, 'Zeebrugge' the glorious naval epic battle as shown to the King and Queen at the Marble Arch Pavilion, 'The Kings Mark' the French classic love story starring Huguette Duflos, 'The Ten Commandments'

Cecil B de Mille's epic. One of the most memorable films in the history of the cinema. Douglas Fairbanks in 'The Thief of Bagdad' and Pola Negri in 'The Spanish Dancer'.

On 2nd April the Newark Choral Society gave a performance of Lobgesang by Mendelssohn. The Musical event of the Season with a choir of 80 voices and orchestra of 30 performers. The live revue show 'London Nights' with Will Harris concluded the spring season. After a summer break the live theatre autumn season opened on Tuesday 15th September with "the World Famous London Star, direct from his American triumphs, the one and only Nelson Keys with a full variety bill." His popularity was reflected in the prices of admission. Dress Circle 5/9d, Orchestra Stalls 4/6d, Upper Circle 3/6d, Saloon 2/4d and Pit 1/2d. It seems curious that the much vaunted dress circle seats which were so expensive are now only in use when the theatre exceeds 400 persons.

This performance was followed by the musical comedy 'Madame Pompadour' with Esme Mayer and Reg Fenton, from George Edwardes', Daly Theatre Production. As usual the warning that patrons are advised to book early heralded a full house. This was followed by Charles Hawtrey's famous farcical comedy 'The Private Secretary', direct from the Playhouse Theatre London starring Lytton Grey and W. A. Mackersby. This was a repeat visit to the Palace. On Monday 5th October the Palace presented 'an evening of extraordinary musical interest'. 'Special visit of World Famous Artistes'. These artists were Peter Dawson, 'the world renowned baritone'. Flora Woodman, 'world famous coloratura soprano' and Beatrice Harrison 'world famous and popular cellist' with Ethel Cook at the piano.

To reassure those patrons that doubted their eyesight the advertisement reaffirms that 'these Great International Artists will positively appear. Prices as for the Nelson Keys concert.' If anyone doubted that this was the Palace's finest season, then the engagement of George Robey, in his prime, with full variety bill, on 23rd October, must have confirmed to everyone that Newark had acquired regional status.

The season was not over. George Robey was followed by Connie Ediss the world famous Gaiety comedienne in the play 'Isobel Edward and Anne' a comedy in three acts. Then came Dorothy Hersee in 'Katya the Dancer' a musical comedy.

Then came the visit of H.M. Band of the Grenadier Guards to give two

Band Concerts. Although the evening performance was full, the matinee audience was not large. The concerts were in aid of the London Association for the Blind. The profits would go to the Duke of Portland's appeal to enlarge the association's workshops which were overcrowded and the Ministry of Health had forbidden the taking of any further blind workers under the existing conditions. Mr Rex Russell the organising Secretary revealed that of the cheques received for the charity all over the country, the highest private individual subscription had come from a resident in the Newark area whose name he was not permitted to disclose.

An interesting competition was held in connection with the concerts. The purchasers of programmes being given the opportunity of guessing the number of people attending both concerts. 1700 guesses were made. Only one guessed the correct number, Mrs Turner 14 Regent St Newark. She won a knitted costume valued at 4½ guineas. The correct attendance was 1,352. This suggests that either some patrons purchased more than one programme or programmes were purchased by non attenders. The profit, which was disclosed on the following Thursday at the Palace Cafe by the Mayor Alderman L. Priestley, was £47. (Receipts £150-9s-6d, expenses £103-9s-6d. Peter the Palace Dog collected £1-3s-8d in his box.

This concert was followed by the musical comedy play 'The Balkan Princess'. On the 3rd December the Newark Choral Society presented 'A Tale of Old Japan' and the Newark Amateur Dramatic Society presented 'Other Peoples Worries' from the 7th-9th December. The London production of 'Cinderella' came on 28th December for six nights and four matinees with C. A. Stephenson as CAPERS?!!

1926 opened with the second pantomime. A bonus in that Cinderella had sold out. This time 'Aladdin' was shown from 11th January until 17th January produced by B. B. and P. H. H. from Burton on Trent. This was followed by 'Kissing Time' which had previously been presented by the Palace in 1923, when this P. G. Wodehouse comedy had sold out. On 5th March The British & Foreign Sailors Society presented the film 'Nelson' at the Palace with proceeds in aid of benevolent funds. Miss Mary Livingstone brought the hilarious farce 'So This Is London' to the Palace for 3 days with Mr. George Ricketts. Musically The Newark Choral Society presented 'Merrie England' and the Band of the Sherwood Foresters gave a Grand Concert. Films in the first half of the year

Mr George Robey, a veteran music hall artist that appeared at the Palace in 1925/26.

included 'The Merry Widow', Ivor Novello in 'The Rat', Emil Jannings as Nero in 'Quo Vadis' and Ronald Colman in 'His Supreme Moment'.

The number of live theatrical productions had declined considerably in the first five months of the year. Coincidentally Cafe opening hours seem to have been reviewed and morning openings discontinued. However the policy of bringing celebrity artistes to Newark continued. On June 11th Josie Collins visited the Palace with her full London Variety Company. Although, like many other artists to appear at the Palace, she is now relatively forgotten. She was hugely popular and is mentioned in the famous Cecily Courtnedge song 'Vitality' as one of the best in the variety age.

The following month on 21st July a flying visit of the world famous star Harry Tate and his London Company direct from the Alhambra and London Coliseum in his latest successes 'Broadcasting' and 'Selling a Car'. Described as the best variety programme ever put on at the Palace. Prices were at the usual celebrity level of 5/9d - 1/3d. On the 16th to 18th August the stage was occupied by the London musical play of 'Cabaret Girl' starring Bobbie Graham and Olive Aubray.

Films took over until the winter season commenced. The best were Douglas Fairbanks in 'Don Q. Son of Zorro' and Rudolph Valentino in 'The Eagle'. Early September brought 'Girl in a Taxi' a play starring Jack O'Shea. On the 19th September a Grand Benefit Concert was held on behalf of Mr B. Curtis Richardson a fellow artist who had prematurely died leaving a widow and children. The augmented Palace orchestra gave its services free and the resultant packed house again showed how Newark cared for its own.

8.   Prior to London

At the end of September the Autumn live productions began with the musical comedy 'Naughty Poppette' previewed at the Palace prior to opening in London. This was followed by the musical comedy from the Duke of York's theatre 'Nicolette'.

On the 2nd November The Band of the Grenadier Guards returned for 2 concerts in aid of the London Association For The Blind. Coincidentally amongst the music played by the military band was selections from 'No No Nanette' which provided an appetiser for the spectacular stage production which arrived the following week at the Palace. The production's band was augmented by several saxophonic players who give us the taste of the Jazz atmosphere which carries the piece all along its adventurous career.

Throughout the early history of the Palace it would be possible to miss several of the unheralded events at the Palace. This was because no comprehensive list of as seasons attractions was made until October 1926. Under the headings 'The Palace Presents', 'Exceptionally Fine Winters Programme' Mr Armstrong states:

"Visitors to Newark who call at the Palace Theatre express admiration not only of the programmmes submitted, but also of the delightful theatre itself and this latter fact is also a pleasant surprise to touring companies who so often have to 'fit up' in Town Halls and the like in much larger towns than Newark, and find in coming to the town a theatre with ample stage space and dressing room accommodation."

He then details the programme and ends with:

"Those who desire good plays and good pictures have no need to journey to Nottingham for the purpose of witnessing them when such an array is presented at Newark's own Theatre."

One item which would never have been noticed was the 6th November afternoon 'Display and Entertainment by five companies of Local Girl Guides'. Another was 'Special Girls Friendly Society'. Film and lecture afternoon only.

The films which were to appear in this winter season were Buster Keaton in 'Go West' 'Blood and Sand' (Rudolph Valentino) 'The Son of the Sheik' also Rudolph Valentino and 'Marion [sic]Lescaunt'!! The odd printers error must occur occasionally. Plays were scheduled up to 4 months ahead. The next event was the Newark Choral Societies Concert entitled 'Gems from the Opera'. Guest soloists were Mr Joseph Farrington (Bass) (BBC and National Opera Company), Miss Gladys Cole (Soprano) and Mr Barrington Hooper (Tenor). This was followed by a return visit of 'Katja the Dancer'. Mrs Lewis Ransome then presented the Newark Dramatic Society in 'Milestones' for three evenings. The musical comedy 'Mercenary Mary' came as a preview to Newark. However this was under a new system that new plays were being toured in the provinces simultaneously with the London Production with a different cast.

The season finished with the new pantomime from Mr Percy H. Holmshaw 'Robinson Crusoe' came for 6 nights and 5 matinees. 'The Most Stupendous and Gorgeous Pantomime ever seen in Nottinghamshire'. It ran from 27th December, had 60 performances, eleven scenes and a special Beauty Chorus of local young ladies. On Xmas day the film showing was Mary Pickford in 'Human Sparrows'.

The first live play of the new year was 'The Last Waltz' for three evenings. This was followed by 'Sunset Land' a fairy play in aid of The Waifs and Strays Society, Mrs Randalls organisation. Also in February was the Newark Choral Society's production of 'Tom Jones' with London artists. Admission prices were now 3/6d, 2/4d and 1/3d. The musical play 'Yvonne' came while the original production was still running at Dalys Theatre London. In March came 'The Last Mrs Cheyney' and 'The Devils Disciple' by G. B. Shaw by the Nottingham Art Theatre. In April Ethel Oliver starred in 'The Street Singer' a musical play. This was followed by a return of 'The Merry Widow'. The final play of the season was 'The Farmers Wife' a Devonshire comedy presented by the Birmingham Repertory Company.

It was commented that the Cafe Suppers and Luncheons were becoming increasingly popular, which shows that the morning closure was really only to enable a better concentration to be made on the evening patrons trade. A one column article on 'Newark's Attractive Cafe' 'How the Palace can please' was placed in the *Newark Herald* on 29th October to entice custom throughout the winter. It gives a comprehensive picture of all aspects of the Cafe at this time. It states:

"How often has the visitor to Newark longed to find a cosy spot where he may enjoy a quiet cup of tea while waiting for a train? How often has a resident longed for somewhere to leave her parcels while shopping, or to refresh herself with a cup of coffee? Or the younger folk, who have wanted a rendezvous for a friend in the evening, where they may sit and talk and smoke over cups of chocolate?

Yet why long for something that is already yours? At the Palace Theatre Cafe all these things you have needed are to be found and there are many other assets to the Cafe—especially for the benefit of patrons— of which many of the patrons know nothing. There is the Cafe itself—approached through a foyer opening into Appletongate, which is the direct route to the L. and N.E. railway station. Comfortable lounges are provided in the foyer, which is as often as not appropriately decorated to harmonise with a picture being shown in the theatre. One day one may find oneself entering a baronial hall of the olden days, and the next a log-cabin when from the windows can be seen vistas of rolling prairie.

Every convenience is at the disposal of visitors to the cafe - well appointed cloak rooms for ladies and gentlemen being provided. Up the wide and carpeted stairs is a room which at once appeals to everyone. There are flowers on the dainty tables, but it is not they which make that appeal: there are spotless cloths toning with the

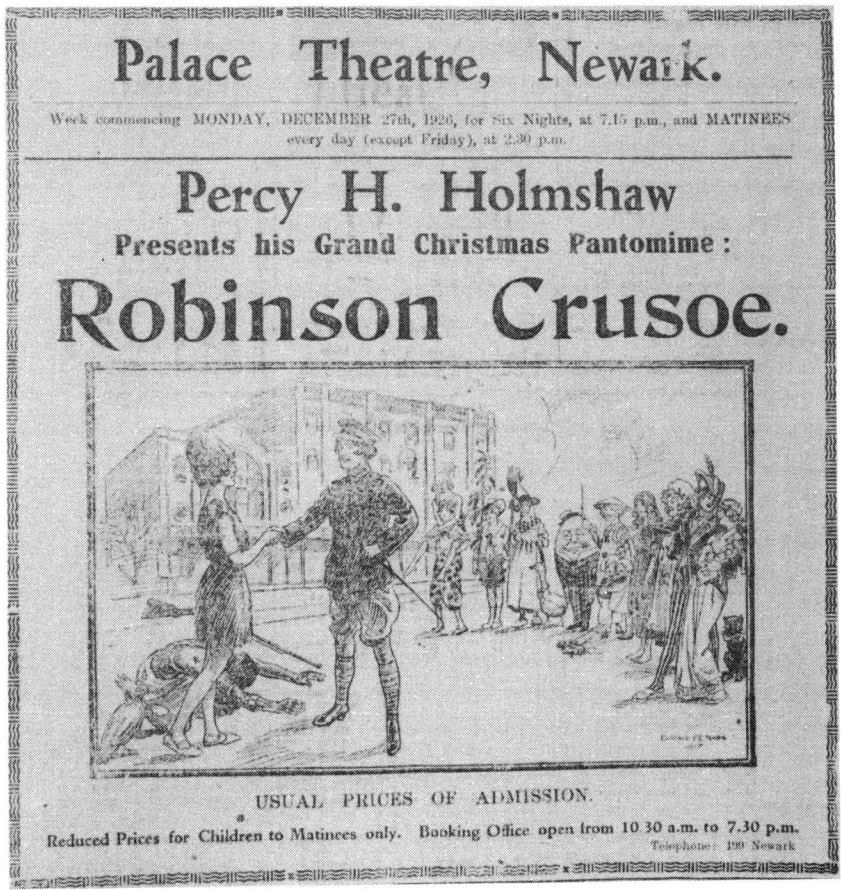

Pantomime poster with Principal Boy dressed in kahki.

curtains at the windows, but it is not they: there are screens—hand-painted years ago—there is mysterious music, there are pictures, but not one of these in itself can make that irresistible appeal. It is the whole that holds some indefinite allurement, a tout ensemble that holds the visitor, and makes him feel that here indeed is that delightful spot for which he has so often wished.

He may think, 'This is indeed a beautiful place, but is utility and service sacrificed for beauty?' It would be quite a natural thought, but one which would be quickly dispelled. Hardly is he seated in one of the comfortable chairs than a neatly-dressed waitress is at his side, his order taken, and there is but time for him to admire for a brief instant the unobtrusive decorations of the cafe, before the meal is placed before him—well cooked, daintily and efficiently served. Three-course luncheons are served every day at 2/-, and customers may have daily, weekly and monthly journals and magazines to read over their coffee.

Another special feature of the cafe is the suppers. Comprising two courses, they are served at 1/6 from 7 o'clock until 9.45 either in the cafe proper or in the theatre at a side table. There is no extra charge for booking a table and the menu is varied and pleasant. To-night, for example, there will be celery soup with toast fingers, cutlets, green peas and potatoes. Rolls, and tea, coffee or chocolate. There are also inclusive theatre and supper tickets at 2/6 comprising a reserved seat in the dress circle and supper served at a reserved table.

During the intervals of a play, light refreshments can be served either in the theatre or in the cafe, and the delicious Palace ices have grown so popular that there is still a great demand for them during the play or the filming of a picture, as well as before the performance or during the intervals.

From the menu and prices of the luncheons and suppers it will be seen that the charges are extremely moderate, and they are in proportion for smaller orders.

During tea the Palace mystery orchestra plays selections and the latest news is, of course, available by wireless.

After tea—or at any time for that matter—there is time for a game of billiards on the full-size billiard table, and the Newark Chess Club, whose headquarters are at the Palace, extend a hearty invitation to temporary members.

It may be mentioned that the Palace has several rooms which are eminently suitable for children's parties, and Miss Ralph, the manageress, will be pleased to quote.

For the convenience of country visitors—and, of course, local residents if they desire to avail themselves of the service—arrangements have been made for parcels to be sent to the Palace from any Newark shop, where they can be called for and so save the trouble of carrying packages about.

There is a car park at the side of the cafe and an up-to-date garage opposite. Patrons also have the use of the public telephone in the office.

There are indeed many more little services which the cafe management has the greatest pleasure in rendering and with them all is the satisfaction of knowing that in every way the Palace is noted for its high standard of quality and neatness—a quality that never varies but always remains the best."

9.   Pavlova - Live on Stage

Summer cinema included Ronald Colman, seen for 6 days in 'Beau Geste'. The live 'All Smiles Revue' with Johnny Clegg opened at Newark prior to London in June. The Yorkshire comedian headed a full variety bill including The Ten Ohio Syncopaters an American dance band and 12 Chorus girls.

In late September the first show of the winter season was the revue 'Nap'. This was followed by the annual visit of the Grenadier Guards on behalf of the blind. At the end of October came the first Chinese film seen in Newark. It was called 'The Legend of the Willow Pattern Plate' and was filmed in China with Chinese actors. The entrepreneurial and financial aspects may have been American. However generally the season was very quiet, yet contains the appearance of the worlds greatest classical dancer Anna Pavlova.

Heralding the visit of Pavlova was the Newark Choral Society production of 'Maritiana' with first class soloists. Anna Pavlova (1881-1931) was born in St Petersburg, entered the Imperial Ballet School in 1891 where the Czar Alexander often inspected or attended a student performance. She always recollected the occasion when the Czar embraced one of her fellow dancers and she burst into tears because 'I wanted the Emperor to kiss me'. Her special talent was noticed by her contemporary Michael Fokine who later became Diaghilev's great revolutionary choreographer and created Pavlova's most famous solo generally known as 'The Dying Swan'.

With the political situation unsure she made her home in London and toured all around the world. When she visited Newark she was approaching 47 years of age. The visit was heralded in the papers from September and the performance was given on Monday 21st November 1927. She appeared with a company of 45 of the Royal Opera House Covent Garden Company. Including Corps and Ballet and a contingent of the Covent Garden Orchestra. Admission prices varied from 12/6d in the Dress Circle to 2/4d unreserved and standing.

"The large audience which comprised people from miles around Newark was thrilled and charmed with the wonderful and inspiring presentations by Madame Pavlova and her company. Never has the theatre rang so loudly, so prolonged, and so frequently with applause as was experienced on Monday and never has an artiste so

The famous dancer - Madame Anna Pavlova

completely captivated a Newark audience as did Anna Pavlova with the beauty of her movements and the quiet appeal of her personality."

A complete analysis of her talents and techniques gives only part of her excellence:

"The real secret must for ever remain unknown: Pavlova herself could not impart it, even if she were willing. You cannot diagnose genius."

She thought that the Palace Theatre was splendid:

"A very good stage for dancing and as regards the structure of the building it is very good for ballet work."

The company manager added:

"The line of sight is excellent. It is one of the best little theatres we have had during the tour from the point of seeing the feet."

When asked 'why should one who can command packed houses at Covent Garden favour a comparatively small audience however appreciative? Her manager said:

"that as an artist she feels she must give her art to the whole world."

The programme presented was exactly the same as that given at Covent Garden with the exception that Newark were given the honour of witnessing a new dance performed for the first time that night. 'Rondino' to the music of Beethoven/Kreisler.

The tour seemed somewhat inhuman. Lasting ten weeks (or 70 days)

" 80 performances will be given throughout the British Isles. Playing in different towns every day and in some cases giving two performances on the same day. For example one day last week a performance was given at York, an evening performance at Scarborough and the company was in Hull the following day. Madame came to Newark from Salford performed at 8 p.m. Left for Oxford at 7.30 a.m. gave a matinee at 3 p.m. and a performance there in the evening at 8 p.m. Madame rehearses every day and with travelling, performing and rehearsals puts in about 18 hours per day. Apart from rehearsals Madame gives a class every day to her dancers being so superb an artist her company must of necessity be trained to the highest pitch to give her suitable support. With such a hectic schedule the nine tons of baggage and scenery to be carried from place to place are facilitated by special transport wagons and special railway arrangements. In fact different programmes were given at different locations so that costumes, scenery and props could be sent to one destination while the others were being used at another. When the tour ended on 10th December she was to commence a tour of Holland, then France and Italy, with an ever larger company. But here she will give a weeks performances in one place."

Undoubtedly Pavlova herself had an immense inner compulsion to dance and a great revulsion at the idea of living beyond the time when she could dance. She, even at 46, was still magnificent while removing certain items from her repertoire (such as The Dragonfly and Valse

Caprice). Her last tour was in 1930 after which she retired to the South of France. While at a New Years party at Cannes a pigeon had flown in through the open window and landed on her shoulder. This disquieted her because of a Russian superstition that such an occurence was an omen of death. The night train on which she was travelling from Cannes to Paris collided with a goods train. While not injured she caught a chill and died on 23rd January 1931, just a week before her fiftieth birthday.

Newark had had an evening to remember. Whatever productions that followed would be inferior. It is ironic that George Robey another of the Palace's great performers is loosely linked with Anna Pavlova. The Pavlova company often encountered a form of moral censorship. There was a disagreeable incident at Birmingham. The local watch committee insisted that one of the girl soloists should wear tights and sandals instead of appearing in bare legs and feet. This inspired George Robey to put stockings on the legs of his grand piano when he appeared in Birmingham.

10. Films Versus Live Theatre

To finish 1927 'Ben Hur' came for 6 days. Three days at the Palace and three days at the Kinema: The Newark Amateur Dramatic Society presented 'Under Cover' a thrilling 'Crook' play and heart throb Ivor Novello had several films at the Palace. The final production in 1927 was in aid of Newark and Nottinghamshire Cripples Hospital School.

1928 opened with the Percy Holmshaw pantomime, produced by Johnny Clegg, 'Babes in the Wood' for 6 nights and three matinees with 14 scenes. Two continental films followed. A two three day showings for the week between The Kinema and the Palace of 'Michael Strogoff' with Ivan Mosjoukine set in Russia by a French film company. This was complemented by the Nordish production of 'The Golden Clown' with Gosta Ekman. The first live drama production since April 1927 was 'The Blue Mazurka' for three evenings from the 23rd January from Daly's London theatre. The relative scarcity of live productions was probably due to the limited three days engagement stipulated by the Palace.

In March the Newark Choral Society presented 'Elijah' with professional principal artists followed by 'What Price Glory' and Fritz Lang's futeristic masterpiece 'Metropolis' featuring Brigitte Helm. On the same page of advertisements for the Palace was 'an important notice'. MacDonald and Young's company in the outstanding success of the generation 'Rose Marie' from Drury Lane London would be appearing at the Palace Newark. The advertisement also contained a booking form for postal applications on its three days engagement 23rd to 25th April. Despite this prompt advert on 7th April advising patrons of this huge live attraction seats were still available on the 21st April. The management placed the following statement in the local paper:-

"Contrary to rumour all seats are not booked at the Palace for Rose Marie on Monday, Tuesday and Wednesday. But you will have to hurry to obtain a good one."

The preview with pictures emphasised the prestige of this production. Seat prices of 3/- Dress Circle and Special Orchestra Stalls, 2/3 Orchestra Stalls and Upper Circle were very reasonable. 'This is not a nondescript show'.

Could it have been that the relative lack of productions had lost a proportion of the live theatre enthusiasts:

"Newark is favoured with its visit largely due to Mr J. W. Armstrong, the Manager of the Palace Theatre, for it is really too big to do two towns in a week. However working in conjunction with Chesterfield it has been arranged, these two towns are the only ones where 'Rose Marie' will run for three nights only. The statistics of the production illustrate the magnitude of the show. Owing to the enormous amount of property travelled the stage setting will have to be started early tomorrow (Sunday) morning in order to get everything ready for the first curtain. Forty stage hands are required and seven electricians for the lighting, the show taking 2 hours and 51 minutes to run including the 15 minutes interval. The Company travels its own orchestra which will be augmented by Palace musicians, making some 16 in all. The musical director from Drury Lane will have a 4 hour rehearsal on Monday. The cast, all understudies of the London production, rehearses twice a week for the producers have a reputation of perfect production which they are not willing to lose. There are nearly 70 players."

At this time a crossroads was reached. It would have been an easy opportunity for a less enthusiastic manager to conclude live professional performances in the Palace especially as additional safety legislation was about to be imposed, raising costs. Mr Armstrong however battled on.

There was no more live professional entertainment until October. During the summer a highly popular short film was 'The Royal Visit to Newark'. The film was shown nightly at both cinemas. The Cafe opened at 3.30 p.m. and 'special wireless music' was heard throughout the Cafe. On 26th September Mr Armstrong applied for stageplay licences to be granted up to January 1929 at Newark County Police Court. Several

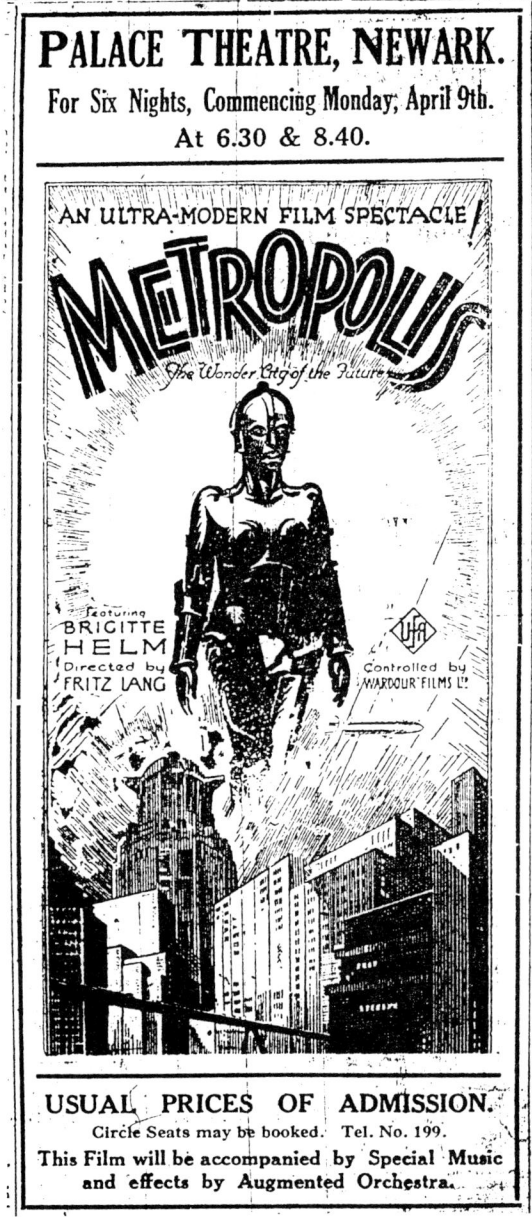

Advertisement for the film Metropolis.

improvements were required before the Licence could be granted and Mr Armstrong promised that they would be put in hand in two or three weeks time. Directors Mr J. H. W. Ford and Mr J. Esam stood as guarantors.

The improvements carried out were:-

"The installation of a fireproof curtain which was to be lowered once during each performance. The exits were to be altered and additional facilities were to be installed for artists leaving the stage and dressing room."

The usual annual Band Concert was held for the Association for the Blind but this time the Band was H.M. Welsh Guards. Live plays returned on the 5th to 10th October with the comedy thriller Arnold Ridley's 'Ghost Train' for 3 evenings.

In November the musical comedy 'Sunny' arrived for 3 evenings direct from London Hippodrome and the Newark Girls High School held its presentation annual speech day during the afternoon. Newark Choral Society presented 'The Messiah' on the 6th December with six principals. J. Bannister Howard sent Ben Travers latest farce 'Thark' produced by Tom Walls from the Aldwych Theatre. The Newark Amateur Dramatic Society presented Ambrose Applejohn's 'Adventure'. The Frodsham Choir gave a concert in aid of the National Childrens Home and Orphanage. Ivor Novello starred in the film of Noel Cowards play 'The Vortex', which with Sybil Thorndike as Edith Cavell provided good film entertainment to close the year.

The year of 1929 opened with the annual pantomime. This time it was 'Dick Whittington and his Cat' with Will A. Jackson. This was followed by the play 'Are You a Mason' in aid of the Newark and District Hospital Ladies Linen Association by local amateurs for three evenings. Special late buses were provided and the Cafe now provided Special Fish Suppers from 7.30 p.m. to 9.15 p.m. at 9d accompanied by wireless selections. The play made a profit of £360, a record amount. The films showing at this time were:- Harry Lauder in 'Huntingtower', Douglas Fairbanks in 'The Gaucho', 'The Last Waltz' adapted from Oscar Strauss' famous musical play.

"The music alone is worth hearing especially as it will be in the capable hands of Mr George Burnley and his fine Palace orchestra."

Dolores Del Rio starred in 'Ramona' for three nights.

"It is a wonderful film and was to have been shown for a week, but owing to the enormous cost its run in Newark had to be curtailed."

Is this the first signs of the rising power of film distributors which gradually dictated more and more to the cinemas?

MacDonald and Young's principal 'Hit the Deck' company brought the famous musical comedy to the Palace for 3 nights commencing Monday 25th February. Patrons were "advised to book as early as possible for this show as there is sure to be a last minute rush for good seats which will not then be obtainable."

"Peggy Petronella about whose death a rumour was broadcast is playing LuLu (Looloo). Far from being dead she is very much alive and is as charming as ever."

Productions such as these were costing the patrons double the admission price of films. Innovations by the manager of obtaining shows which performed two houses and consequently halved the cost ensured the continuance of live entertainment.

In April the Newark Choral Society performed 'Faust' on the 9th of April with BBC radio artists as principals including Megan Thomas, Walter Flynn and Foster Richardson.

11.   In The Shadow of the Talkie

The summer presented a lively selection of entertainment. The first week in May Harry Benets brilliant company in 'Once in a Blue Moon', a pierrotic fantasy by a super Concert Party. At the head of the cast were Palace favourites Mr Vivian Foster 'The Vicar of Mirth' and Mr Richard Teasdale who visited the Palace in 'No No Nanette' and 'Mercenary Mary'. Lower down the bill was the beautiful Sally Gray who was to star in many British films until the end of the Second World War. Mr Armstrong predicted capacity houses. There would be two houses nightly and a complete change of programme for the second half of the week. Prices were as films 1/6 Circle, 1/- Saloon, 6d pit.

Week commencing 17th June had the *extra special attraction* of Max Erand and his £5,000 Cathedral Organ, suported by Welsh Tenor Mr David Williams and the famous French Medium Yvonne Astra. Max Erand appeared at most principal theatres. Costing £300 per week the Palace needed capacity houses since 2 full scale films Pola Negra in 'Loves of an Actress' Monday to Wednesday and Esther Ralson in 'Half a Bride' completed the programme. The organ weighed 14 tons and needed 5 railway trucks to transport it.

"Madame Yvonne tells you all you wish to know. She answers unseen questions. Simply write your questions, Astra gazes into her magic crystal and gives you the answer. Astra may be consulted privately at the Theatre from 10 a.m. to 5 p.m. and during the Evening Performance." Perhaps the Palace management consulted her regarding the imminence of talking pictures?

On the first of July for three days came Al Jolson in 'The Jazz Singer'. However this was the silent version. All of the previews and descriptions of Jolson 'possessed of considerable histrionic ability, a most unusual musical show. Versatility in the way of song and dance, above all a gift for delivering lines' The engagement of Mr Brookes Marsden the celebrated Yorkshire baritone to "sing" at the theatre during the film' can only have frustrated the audience who wanted Jolson to sing.

From July 22nd to 24th the Palace presented the Russian Ballet 'an enormous attraction'. 'Londons latest rage' 'direct from the Royal Opera House, Covent Garden and His Majesty's Theatre'. It starred several Diaghilev dancers, the most famous being Stanizles Idzikowski, who created a furore in New York, Paris and London in 'Harlequin' and Spirit of the Rose, also Vera Savina and Vanda Edvina. Like Pavlova's company three quarters of the dancers were British, some assuming Russian names but most retaining their own names, Marjorie Daw, Phylis Stickland and Juliette Phylimore. The company of 30 artistes presented a more contemporary approach than Pavlova who at the end of her career was thought by Diaghilev to be somewhat old fashioned.

They performed 'La Spectre de la Rose', 'Bluebird Dancers', 'Chinese Porcelain', 'Les Sylphides', 'The Fire Dance', 'Siamese Goddess' and 'Grand Divertissement'.

With admission prices of Dress Circle/Special Orchestra Stalls 5/9d, Upper Circle and Orchestra Stalls 3/6d, Saloon 2/4d and Pit 1/6d for three performances the Palace was taking a huge gamble.

In August came Edgar Wallace's 'The Ringer' a thriller play which came for 3 nights 19-21 August with 2 performances each evening, with H. Hodgson Bentley as Dr Lomond, as at Wyndhams Theatre London. This was followed by 'Captivating Kitty' a musical comedy from the Duke of York's Theatre London.

"In order to give everyone an opportunity of seeing the comedy the management is arranging for a twice nightly show at 6.30 and 8.40, prices will be 1/6d, 1/- and 9d."

A most popular film was 'Royal Remembrances' showing some of the earliest films to the current days, including Kitchener's return from South Africa, the Coronation of King Edward, King Edwards funeral, the Coronation of King George, Queen Victoria's state visit to Dublin. Queen Victoria's funeral and 'The First Gordon Bennett race'!

The winner of the first Oscar as best picture in 1928 was 'Wings' starring Clara Bow and Richard Arlen and came to the Palace at the end of August.

In October Miss Clarice Mayne headed a variety bill from 21st until 23rd October. Admission prices had increased to 2/- Circle, 1/3d Saloon and 6d pit. She had been the wife and partner of the late Mr James Tate whose double turn on the Halls as 'This and That'. She had been a principal boy in Pantomime and now was presenting a new entertainment assisted by her pianist. 'She will be supported by a galaxy of talent'. The article continues with:-

"The experiment of two houses a night has proved this week that the management has sensed the need of the play going public of Newark. Many people, however, on Monday, Tuesday and Wednesday seeing a large queue gave up hopes of getting a seat and returned home. Patrons are asked to remember that the Palace has a seating capacity of 1,260 and it would take a queue from the Palace to Beamond Cross to fill it. If, therefore there is a queue to Magnus buildings patrons can still be assured a comfortable seat even if they are at the end of the line of waiting playgoers.

This variety bill was followed by the comedy play 'Alf's Button' by W. A. Darlington. This concerned a magic brass button which, when rubbed, produced a genie. It became quite famous and spawned several sequels on film. In November came Mrs Ernest Randall's production of 'Our Flat' a farcial comedy by Mrs Musgrove in aid of the Waifs and Strays. Prices were 3/-, 2/3d, 1/3d and 9d. Buses will run from all surrounding villages. This was followed by the Newark Choral and Orchestral Society's Autumn Concert. Admission prices from 4/6d. It presented Coleridge Taylor's 'Hiawatha' followed by a second half concert by the principals both vocal and instrumental. The chorus and orchestra numbered 140. This was the first appearance of the newly created orchestra.

The Newark Girls High School again held their annual Speech Day at the Palace and Edgar Wallace's play 'The Terror' performed for three nights to excellent audiences. This was followed by the Newark Amateur Dramatic Society's production of 'The Sport of Kings' from 2nd to 4th

December. Admission prices were 3/- to 9d.

12. The End of an Era

1930 opened with the pantomime 'Cinderella'. It was to be the last for 23 years. However the year continued unaware of the vast differences talking pictures would bring.

The play 'Interference' came at the end of January from St James' Theatre London. From 3rd to 5th February a return visit of the musical comedy 'Irene'. On the 17th February the Ballard Brown Revue 'Very Good Very Good' was presented twice nightly for the week. In the cast were Will Fyffe's daughters 'The Sisters Fyffe'. This was followed by a musical war play 'The Better 'Ole'.

Opening the month of March was 'A Great Musical Novelty' 'something as good if not better than the talkies'. This ambitious claim heralded 'Laughter and Tears' 'The great human talkie' drama. The film featuring Little Pearl Hay is accompanied and synchronised by the Four Melody makers, Miss Elsa Worth (Soprano), Miss Ada Worthington (Contralto), Mr A. E. Roberts (Tenor) and Mr Eric Taylor (Baritone). Some of the songs featured were:- 'Somewhere a Voice is Calling', 'Ave Maria (Gounod's), 'My Ain Folk', 'Bonnie Mary of Argyle', 'Love's Old Sweet Song', 'Sanctuary of the Heart', 'Where My Caravan Has Rested', 'Annie Laurie', 'Coming Through The Rye' and 'Home Sweet Home'. The supporting feature was the silent film 'The Letter':

Also in March came the Aldwych Theatre farce by Ben Travers 'Rookery Nook'. The Newark Choral and Orchestral Spring offering was 'King Olaf' containing 150 local performers, 3 vocal stars and four star instrumentalists. The famous vocal stars in this Edward Elgar masterpiece were Isobel Baillie (Soprano), Parry Jones (Tenor) and Howard Fry (Bass). This was a special en route engagement, the first appearance in Nottinghamshire.

In the film 'Piccadilly' a minor actor in the cast was hailed as a future British film star "if only he will come over to the movies." He was at this time starring in the title role of Mr Pickwick at the Haymarket Theatre London. His name was Charles Laughton.

The last live production before the talkies came was the variety show 'Clock The Laughs'. It was classed as 'a New Type Road Show'. Joe

Boganny was at the top of the bill after 3 command performances before their majesty's the King and Queen. Also on the bill were Mark Griver and his Scottish Revellers the famous band from the Palladium London, The Garlic Quartet from Moscow and full supporting bill.

A good AGM was held at the Palace and the purchase of the Corn Exchange was completed.

Chapter 3

THE TALKIES - 1930-39

1.   The Talkies Arrive

On 15th March 1930 under the heading of 'The Talkies are Coming' the management of the Palace Theatre have pleasure in announcing that talkie films will shortly be introduced and a Western Electric Sound Projection System will be installed. The first film to be shown and heard will be 'Broadway Melody', the world famous singing and dancing film. The local press congratulated the Palace management on bringing this latest invention so early in the talkie history

> "Once seen these pictures have an irresistable attraction. Those responsible have not only sensed the taste of the public but have also shown a commendable urge to provide Newark with the latest and best."

So on Easter Monday (21st April) will see the first showing of the Talkies in Newark. *The Herald* representative visited the Palace and

> "found an army of electricians and others busily engaged in installing the apparatus under the keen eye of a highly qualified electrical engineer of the Western Electric Company. These systems have cost as much as £7,000 to install. Behind the stage was seen a mountain of boxes of all sizes 22 in number each containing some component part awaiting the master hand and mind to assemble, the amplifiers, springs sprockets, valves, tubes diaphrams, coils etc., into a perfect whole.
> The new projection machines are housed in the present projector room which has been enlarged. These machines will be capable of dealing with the two types of talkies, sound on film and sound on disc. From the projecting room will run the connecting wires which carry the sound to the back of the screen. Here will be erected 2 huge steel towers of 18 ft each which will carry two giant loudspeakers five feet square. These throw the sound directly on to the pictures on a screen with minute holes which, while not discernible have the effect of allowing the sound to come uninterrupted from the horns into the cinema."

Prices of admission were Dress Circle (first 2 rows) 1/6d, Circle 1/3d, Special Saloon 1/-, Saloon 9d, pit 6d. This, thanks to technology, was actually cheaper than the prices of the opening night of the Palace Theatre nearly 10 years before. Newark Cinemas Ltd. as a matter of caution kept silent films running at the Kinema:

> "There are those patrons who prefer the calm quietude which seemed to pervade the

pictures and in catering for this class of picturegoer the Kinemas popularity should go on undiminished."

This ensured a retention of the 'splendid orchestra' which will give of its best under the direction of the delightful violin maestro Madam Cooper. The Palace Theatre Orchestra has now gone. Mr George Burnley was retained as sound engineer. The programme of silent films starred Victor McLaglen, Ivor Novello, John Gilbert, Buster Keaton, Wallace Beery, Ramon Novarro and Joan Crawford. A special augmented orchestra was used in 'The King of the Khyber Rifles' at the Kinema. But people flocked to the Palace and were urged to book their seats to avoid disappointment.

Amongst the excellent quality films were Norma Shearer in 'The Last Mrs Cheyney', from the world famous play seen at the Palace in 1927 also 'The Desert Song', 'John Boles', 'The Hollywood Revue', with 25 great stars and a chorus of 200. Al Jolson in 'The Singing Fool' (the film that started the talkies) and 'Gold Diggers of Broadway'.

So popular were the films that at the end of September a notice was advertised that:

"Patrons who intend to visit the Palace on Mondays, Thursdays and Saturdays are advised to book their seats to avoid disappointment."

For the comfort of patrons, to prevent deterioration, internal flooding and to proclaim the new talking pictures an awning was erected along the outer pavement on the left hand side of the theatre as far as the fire exit. Joining the awning was a canopy across the Palace entrance which, I am told, stated Palace Theatre Talking pictures.

The Kinema had now turned back to music variety to augment its silent programmes. Examples were The Three Musical Valeroes (musical melange), The Great Hillards (magic feats), Percy Pryde with his phono fiddle, and Val Vett the ragtime rag picking rag painter. Some of whom would disrupt the 'calm quietude'. Inevitably talkies were introduced using the BTH 'talkie' apparatus. It was hoped that it would foster the British Thomson-Houston Company, which was in manufacture by 8th December 1930.

The silent film show was now dead. Reflecting upon the last decade the five reelers vanished and gradually epic films arose which despite the strange physical acting style could be termed great. It was in 1930 a completed apprenticeship. No longer would a glance be needed to convey emotions (and also save a few dollars on subtitles). Nazimova with her "1000 moods" must have saved a fortune.

As an epitaph to that era "I salute Alla Nazimova (1879-1945) Russian Actress who in 1904 was the leading lady of a St Petersburg Theatre. She toured Europe and America and in 1906 having learnt English in less than six months appeared as Hedda Gabler at the Princess Theatre New York. She remained in America where she was considered an outstanding exponent of Ibsens heroines and in 1910 appeared at the Nazimova Theatre (The Thirty Ninth St Theatre) demolished in 1925.

After some years in films she returned to the stage playing with the Civic Repertory Company in Ibsen, Chekhov, Turgenev and O'Neill. Newark's first screen Goddess. Although her early films have been lost she can be seen prominently in the classic "Blood and Sand" 1941 remake starring Tyrone Power, Rita Hayworth, Linda Darnell and Anthony Quinn.

The quality of the films were also a threat to live theatre. Excellent stories could be told with heroic star actors and actresses making excellent use of beautiful locations with close ups, background music and other devices to make them superior for most people to a provincial play. Importantly they were half the price of live theatre. Sir Donald Wolfit admits

"with the arrival of the 'talkies' matters in the theatre and especially in the provinces were in a serious state. The shadow of Al Jolson as the 'Singing Fool' hung over theatreland.

The Palace policy was to choose the better of the available films.

"Some of the attractions we have for the future rank amongst the finest talking pictures ever produced"

said Mr Armstrong the manager. He added

"that unpleasant American twang (accent) has been absolutely eliminated from them."

Those were the days. Among the presentations was Norma Shearer in 'Their Own Desire' and 'At the Villa Rose'. The cast included Richard Cooper who appeared in person at the Palace in the play 'Lord Richard in the Pantry'. 'Paris' featuring Jack Buchanan, 'Rookery Nook' with Tom Walls. Incidentally the stage version visited the Palace in 1930 being the last professional live play to be seen at the Palace. As always the Palace presented good British films when available. "Blackmail" Alfred Hitchcock. "The Berg" which was the story of the Titanic'.

The silent movie and stage actress Alla Nazimova.

2. Local Societies to provide Live Theatre

The first live play at the Palace after the coming of the talkies was "The Cheerful Knave" on Monday 8th December for 3 evenings and one matinee presented by the Newark Amateur Dramatic Society. Unfortunately no pantomime was engaged. The loss of the orchestra must have been a factor in the decision. On the 26th January 1931 Mrs Ernest Randall presented "Lord Richard in The Pantry" for the Mount School rebuilding fund, it ran for 3 days including a matinee.

In April Greta Garbo starred in 'Romance'. Paul Whiteman and his band starred in 'The King of Jazz' for 6 days. The film that was most popular for about 40 years was 'All Quiet on the Western Front' with Lew Ayres. The local papers warned patrons that owing to the immense popularity of Norma Shearer in 'Divorce' it would be adviseable to book their seats no later than 3 o'clock for either the 6.30 or 8.40 performances.

In May 'The Blue Angel' with Emil Jannings and Marlene Dietrich arrived. It was shown on regional television in 1993. A benefit concert was arranged for George Burnley the ex musical director and lately sound manager. Perhaps the adaptation to a new rôle proved somewhat disagreeable. Charlie Chaplin's 'City Lights' came for 6 nights in October and the Ideal Cinema opened in Southwell.

On the 23rd November for 3 nights the Newark Amateur Dramatic Society presented 'Nine-Forty-Five'. Seats were priced at 3/-, 2/4d, 1/3d and 6d. On the 27th November for 5 nights the play 'Spring Cleaning' was performed in aid of the Newark Ladies Linen Association and Prevention of Cruelty to Children.

1932 opened with John Barrymore in 'Svengali' and Barbara Stanwyck in '10 Cents a Dance'. On Sunday 28th February The Newark Borough Band gave a Charity concert at the Palace with soloists and monologues. Priced at 1/- and 6d a good house was reported.

On the 20th March the last Sunday concert of the season was given at the Palace Theatre by the British Legion Band. It was noticeable that several local societies were holding events elsewhere. "Coils" at the Technical College, Newark Choral at the Town Hall, Leicester Fortune Players performing Shakespeare at the Town Hall.

On 22nd June a missionary film entitled 'Palestine' was shown at 3 p.m., 6 p.m. and 8.10 p.m. Views of the Middle East were personally described by the Producer T. H. Baxter FRCS.

Although a variety of dances had been held in the early twenties from tea to evening dances, from jazz to popular dances, no attempt had been made to teach dancing. The local news on 17th September featured the New Dance Room,

"'Palace Theatre Innovation'.

The news, which will be particularly welcome to devotees of Terpsichore, reflects the enterprise of the Palace management and patrons who have not yet had a prior view of the little hall, which is really an annexe to the cafe, will be charmed with its cosiness and general suitability.

On the opening night there will be dancing from 7-11 p.m. and the hostess and instructress will be Nancy Clarke M.A.O.D., M.I.S.T.D., H.B.B.O., of The Studio, Mikado Cafe Nottingham, who will have the help of her two lady assistants. Miss Clarke will be in attendance to answer enquiries and to make appointments from 3 p.m. on Thursday afternoons throughout the winter. The charges will be very moderate. There is no doubt that the new venture will fill a want in Newark."

The initial advertisement stated that "dancing was to be held every Thursday and Saturday from 3 p.m. when Miss Clarke would be in attendance. The Saturday evening dance admission price was 1/6d. Then dancing sessions would be held every afternoon and evening from 3 p.m. Special Evening Dress nights are being arranged also combined tickets to enable patrons to visit the pictures, have supper and dance.

Distinct success attended the opening of the new Palace Dance room on Thursday night 22nd September 1932 and the venture promises to meet the requirements of many in Newark and district who have long felt the need of such a room. Although the weather was against it, a large number of dancers assembled to meet Miss Nancy Clarke the charming hostess who was accompanied by a number of visitors from Nottingham.

The room is particularly cosy, and having an excellent floor should prove a popular rendezvous for lovers of good dancing. During the evening exhibitions of ballroom dancing were given by Miss Sylvia Widdowson (AISTD) and Miss Peggy Soames (MBBO) 'Miss Clarke's assistants'. At all the dances hostesses will always be in attendance to partner and introduce dancers. Miss Clarke is arranging lessons and classes in ballroom, character and tap dancing."

Although adverts continued for several months the initiative does not seem to have been long standing. Times were hard in Newark. *The Herald* reviewed 'Hunger Marches in Newark'. Mrs. Ernest Randall continued her Charity productions on behalf of the Waifs and Strays. Her Autumn presentation was 'The Windmill Man' at the Palace for 6 days from 24th October. Prices from 3/- to 1/-. It was reported that the Saturday matinee when prices were cheapest, was a sell out and 'many failed to gain admittance'. A sign of the times was that although the cheaper seats were sold out many of the dearer seats were vacant. John Wayne starred in 'The Virtuous Wife' showing 10th September.

It was left to the amateur societies to provide live entertainment at the Palace. On the 28th November for 3 days the Newark Amateur Dramatic Society presented 'A Damsel in Distress' by Ian Hay and P. G. Wodehouse, in aid of the Newark District Nursing Association and St Catherine's Home.

The first live event in 1933 was on Sunday the 8th of January. A popular Concert was presented by the British Legion in aid of branch funds. Admission was modest at '1/- upstairs and 6d below'.

Probably to appease the lovers of live theatre and with the birth pains of the talkies over, the management of the Palace advertised 'an enormous attraction'. Leon Underwood presented the famous musical play from the Lyric and Dalys Theatres London, Schuberts 'Lilac Time' from 27th February for 3 nights. Prices were relatively modest (Dress Circle 3/6d, Upper Circle 2/-, Special Stalls 3/-, Stalls 2/-, Saloon 1/-). It contained the entire production as presented in London with augmented Orchestra and large expensive Company. If this succeeded then perhaps the great days of the Palace would be revived. The show was a success

> "That Newark appreciates a change from a continuous round of 'talking pictures' is illustrated by the large audiences which flocked to see 'Lilac Time'. The company received a hearty reception and the hope was expressed on all sides that further opportunity for similar entertainment will be afforded. Newark will be humming with these well known airs for some time and people who have not visited the Palace to see this excellently produced, well mounted and prettily dressed play depicting the story of Schubert must make a point of seeing the show tonight."

The weekly advertisement for the Palace also contained the phrase 'Dance room available for Private Dances, Parties, whist Drives, meetings etc.,' which suggested that the Nancy Clarke dances had ceased.

Mrs Ernest Randall produced many charity shows for Newark.

On Sunday the 9th March a further British Legion Concert was held.

In May Miss Ralph, Cafe Manageress since June 1920, decided to leave the Palace.

"The many friends of Miss Ralph and particularly cafe patrons will regret to learn that she is leaving Newark to take up a position of Manageress of the White Hart Hotel Lincoln. During her employment she has demonstrated her splendid artistic abilities in the decoration of the Cafe and of the foyer where her dainty and artistic models have been much admired."

From 1926 the Cafe hours of opening had been reduced. The Cafe no longer opened for mornings beginning at 12.00. This indicates that the level of patronage had declined with the loss of the major live shows. Worse was yet to come. In July the Cafe only opened at 3.30 p.m.. In October the Cafe menu advertised only Light Refreshments.

On 20th October Vice Admiral Gordon Campbell presented a thrilling lecture occupying the usual first house picture times with 'My Mystery Ships' at 7 p.m. prompt. Prices were 3/-, 2/- and 1/- in aid of the Newark Hospital. Patrons were advised to book early.

In November the Palace hosted the Newark Girls High School Speech Day and the Newark Amateur Dramatic Society presented the Agatha Christie thriller 'Alibi' from 27th to 29th in aid of the Unemployed Welfare and Nursing Association.

The year had been unhappy for the Palace. The new era of change occasioned by the advent of talking pictures, was beginning to show. In doubt were the lavish London productions, the style and excellence of the catering and the magnificent surroundings which had drawn the cream of the district to the Palace. This mingling of the devotees exuded a unique atmosphere created and fostered by the Manager Mr J. Armstrong and Miss Ralph who as catering manageress also artistically decorated the leisure areas creating an aesthetic atmosphere.

Practically every touring Company praised all aspects of the stage and staff. Charles Doran said that Mr Armstrong, a theatre devotee, had practically created a number one touring venue in a number two town.

The provision of talkie equipment was costly but the resulting product of an unlimited stream of excellent films containing outdoor locations, action, beautiful scenery, a cast of thousands and starring the cream of the stage stars and new American matinee idols and love goddesses. All at half the price of a touring theatre production.

The ease of showing regular films made the setting up, operating and dismantling of a company seem a Herculean task. What with the Palace costs of keeping stage equipment current and in good order and the continual expansion of safety precautions the continuance of live theatre was inperilled.

The success of 'Lilac Time' probably created more problems than it solved since no other professional productions appeared in the next few months. The Cafe hours were reduced firstly from 12 hours to 9½ hours then to 6½ hours suggesting that some aspects of the Palace were losing money. With an era of mass unemployment caution was in the air. Miss Ralph's departure followed in November by Mr Armstrong's, left the decision of future live shows very much in doubt.

> "Much of the success of this popular picture house is due to his tactfulness and geniality. Apart from watching over the interests of his company and the comfort of Palace patrons, he has given a great deal of time and the benefit of his experience on behalf of charity, and the various organisations, dramatic and otherwise, which have used the Palace for their productions in aid of good causes, have found him a willing helper."

The reason given for his departure was that the recent expansion of the Robin Hood Hotel and the consequent increase in business. This had made it impossible for Mr Armstrong (who had been the licensee since 1920) to continue the dual offices. But was it? Had Mr Armstrong and Miss Ralph realised that the talkies had created a new world to which they could not be reconciled. Undoubtedly they worked in harmony. I am told that some wag solemnly placed an advertisement in the local newspaper proclaiming their future marriage. Fortunately this mischevious item was discovered before publication, and burnt.

This year of leaving's became more poignant when Mr Harold Snushall Chief Cinema Operator at the Kinema died at the age of thirty leaving a wife of eighteen months. Newark Cinemas Ltd staff lined the path of the church in tribute.

On 23rd December the Thomas Magnus School held its Speech Day at the Palace. Films of the year included Humphrey Bogart in 'Love Affairs', Norma Shearer, who appears to have taken the mantle of Nazimova, Frederick March and Leslie Howard in 'Smilin Through', Bette Davis in 'The Dark Horse', 'Grand Hotel' with Greta Garbo and John Barrymore. Jack Payne and his band 'Say It with Music'.

On the 3rd January 1934 an advertisement of a Sunday Evening Concert on 28th January appeared in aid of the Poor Children's Boot fund organised by Police Inspector M. H. Bolt and Mrs C. E. Parlby. 400 tickets had already been sold. The Principal artiste was to be Mr Donald Wolfit in selected items from his repertoire. Miss J. Vincent Robinson in violin solos accompanied by Madame d'Ascanio, Mrs Stanley Cooling of Lincoln (Operatic Soprano) and 'The Melody Three' from the Bradford City Police Fund and artistes from Huddersfield to be named later. Tickets 2/- and 1/- from members of the Newark Borough Police. One wonders if this is why 400 tickets had already been sold.

The indefatigable Mrs Ernest Randall presented a type of pantomime 'Bluebell in Fairyland' from the 8th to 13th January in aid of the Newark Cripples Guild.

The Clinton Arms placed an advertisement in the Advertiser for 'After Theatre & Pictures Suppers'.

"The proprietor begs to remind patrons that the coffee room remains open for late suppers. Alcoholic refreshments served with a meal may be ordered up to eleven oclock on week days. It would materially assist service if you would order your meal before 10 p.m. and so ensure everything being in readiness on your arrival after the show."

This seems to suggest a further decline in the provision of food by the Palace Cafe.

3.   The Wolfit Drama Week

The 24th January copy of the *Newark Advertiser*, 4 days before the Concert, had an open letter from Donald Wolfit. He heads it with 'Suggestion for Drama Festival in Newark'.

"Will the people of Newark come to their Theatre to support a company of London actors and actresses in a week of Drama if given the opportunity? Would they care to have presented to them in one week the joyous comedy of 'Twelfth Night' (Shakespeare), the biting wit and satire of George Bernard Shaw's 'Arms on the Man', the magnificent tragedy of 'The Master Builder' by one of the foremost dramatists of the world Henrik Ibsen whose work has never been performed in Newark, to my knowledge. Would they come not once, but three or more times during the week. If they feel disposed to support such a week of drama which will entail much labour and thought, I am prepared to do my humble best to present these plays to them in as worthy a manner as is possible with the help of the local management sometime in the near future."

The Donald Wolfit Drama Week including, Donald Wolfit, Margaret Rutherford and local actor Sydney Vere Laurie.

The concert was a tremendous success and a profit of £100 was made, the Directors of Newark Cinemas lending the theatre and staff for the evening. It was announced that

"Mr Wolfit is to bring a Company in April to present a Drama week for Newark. Special scenery will be brought from London. In order to quicken interest in the Wolfit week a local committee will be formed from representatives of local organisations. A drama competition will be organised for the schools and for this a shield is being offered by the Directors of the Palace Theatre."

A lecture was given on Ibsen at the technical college to encourage interest in the Drama week.

While corresponding to G. B. Shaw on financial matters Donald Wolfit, to promote the festival, requested him to send a message to the people of Newark. His reply was not as expected. The famous man wrote

I bar messages. My life would not be worth living if I started that game. Besides, the inhabitants of Newark on Trent are quite intelligent enough to take it for granted that I wish success on any enterprise when my plays are in the bill, faithfully G. Bernard Shaw.

The Drama week was to commence on 9th April 1934 and the following artists engaged.

Margaret Webster; the daughter of the great acting couple Ben Webster and Dame May Whitty; one of the most promising actresses on the London Stage. She will play Viola, Hilda and Louka. Alfred Harris an old Bensonian, will appear as Sir Toby Belch. Frank Milray, Elspeth March, Alfred Sangster and local boy Sidney Vere-Laurie. Also Margaret Rutherford, who became a household name and a Dame, and Molly Hartley Milburn.

The 4th April edition of the *Newark Advertiser* contained photographs of Donald Wolfit, Dorothy Green, Margaret Webster, Margaret Rutherford and Sidney Vere-Laurie. The cast was completed by Dorothy Green, Jack (later Sir John) Clements, Laurier Lister, Frank Darch and Charles Hickman.

The weeks performances were Monday and Tuesday 'Arms and The Man' (G. B. Shaw), Wednesday and Thursday 'The Master Builder' (Ibsen) and Friday and Saturday afternoon and evening 'Twelfth Night' (Shakespeare).

Prices were season tickets 7/6d and 5/6d and individual performances 3/-, 2/- and 1/-. The Free List was suspended. Children half price for the Saturday matinee. Performances commenced at 7.15. Mr Wolfits billing was three times larger than anyone elses. He describes his first venture into actor-management.

> "What was more natural than to think in terms of actor management, conducting my own company and soaring to unknown heights on wings of fire? One great obstacle to this ambition was the lack of sinews of war: I had no wealthy friends and the shadow of Al Jolson as 'The Singing Fool' hung over theatreland. Nonetheless I proposed a Drama week at Newark. A small guarantee was forthcoming from the town and for one glorious week I gave my home audience a taste of my quality as Bluntschli in 'Arms and the Man', as Solness in 'The Master Builder' and finally as Malvolio in 'Twelfth Night'.
>
> Looking back on the programme of 'unknown names' it is interesting to find that I presented the following now famous artists in that exciting week: Margaret Rutherford, John Clements, Elspeth March, Alfred Sangster (author of the Brontes) and Margaret Webster who has given America a great series of Shakespeare revivals in the last decade or so. The production of 'The Master Builder' in modern dress was presented at the Westminster Theatre in London on our return and two weeks later at the Embassy Theatre for a short run."

The critics were warm in their praise and the performance was described as Ibsen without boredom. One reviewer said that 'anything like a first class performance of Ibsen was such a rarity that the present production ought to be one of London's outstanding attractions'. So Newark had two Knights and a Dame of the theatre for a week and Donald Wolfit was on his way as an actor manager.

The lack of finance led to various local measures. 'After each performance the cast hurried home to their kind host and hostesses' who provided their keep for the week. It was commented that some of the temporary hosts thought this an honour and cause of much excitement.

The gossip column "Castle Wall" acknowledged a major Wolfit triumph

> "the town will go back to its pictures and will feel that all work and no *play* makes Jack a dull boy."

It was a case of O to be in Newark now that the April Drama week is there.

Mr Jack Cann, newly made manager on the departure of Mr Armstrong, said that 'he will relish the peace of the talkies'.

The next live event was not until Sunday the 28th October when Constance Shacklock (Contralto) headed the bill in the Colliery Disaster Benefit Concert. Occasioned by the Gresford Pit disaster. Commencing at 7.45. Tickets 2/- and 1/-, a profit of £50 resulted.

The film 'Damaged Lives' was shown from the 8th to 10th of November showing 3 times daily, 3 p.m., 6.30 p.m. and 8.40 p.m. It was shown under the auspices of the British Social Hygiene Council. 'An astonishing exposé of humanity's greatest problems'. Over 16s only. Presumably patrons became extremely wary of toilet seats over the next few weeks. The subject of course V.D.

More familiar films of the year were 'King Kong', a major step forward in film animation, an 18 inch model Kong seen as large as the skyscrapers. Charles Laughton in 'The Private Lives of Henry VIII' for six days also in the bill the 'Baer-Carnera World Title Heavyweight fight' and 'Riptide' Norma Shearer and Robert Montgomery.

1935 was a tremendous year for films. On 2nd of January 'Queen Cristina' came for a week starring Greta Garbo and John Gilbert. The following week Gracie Fields in 'Sing as We Go'. All week the free list was suspended and an extra matinee on Wednesday at 3 p.m. was arranged.

4.   Threat of Competition

On the 23rd January the announcement of the establishment of a new super cinema on a site in Middlegate was the last news that Newark Cinemas needed. In such a small town advance notice would have been received and defensive measures planned, one of which was to show the best films available. By the 30th January a site had been secured by Newark Cinemas 'for the purpose of erecting a new cinema which will be conveniently situated for the increasing population on that side of the town.

The site was Bow Villa the London Road property of Councillor Ernest Randall. The site did not include the bowling green and surrounding gardens. On the 6th February the new cinema in Middlegate was named The Savoy. On the 13th February under the heading 'Yet another site for a Cinema' Newark Cinemas announced that a site in Lombard Street had been purchased some time ago from Clifford A. T. Lawrence as a speculative site at some future time.

Newark Cinemas presented plans to Nottinghamshire County Council for alterations to the Corn Exchange purchased in 1930. Thus several guns had been fired across the bows of the Savoy Cinema. Owners warning of a war of attrition. Meanwhile on this Machiavellian week Eddie Cantor led the 'Roman Scandals' at the Palace.

On the 3rd March the charity Newark Infirmary Wireless Fund held a benefit. It was a Sunday Grand Variety Concert with the Nottingham Accordian Band at 7.45 p.m. Prices 2/6 - 1/-.

On the 20th March Donald Wolfit's letter to the editor of the *Newark Advertiser* was published. He suggested a second Festival for this Jubilee Year. He would be ready for a week in Newark about the third week in May if dates can be arranged.

> "Mr Wolfit will make no plans until he hears whether another week will be acceptable but he feels that a second effort would receive more support because Newark people realise that he would bring a first class company."

Which suggested that last years attendances were not sufficient to guarantee a profit. It was an inopportune time. However little or however much Newark Cinemas had wished to help they needed every penny to fight the new super cinema on their doorstep. On the 27th 'The Barretts of Wimpole Street' came to the Palace for a week (and an extra matinee) starring Charles Laughton, Norma Shearer and Frederick March. The film of the play that Wolfit had in mind bringing to Newark. The comparisons of cinema versus stage would have been artistically and financially worth comparison.

Early in April Emily Blagg died with her Palace still the Premier Cinema in Newark and her Kinema still bringing in the audiences.

Meanwhile blockbuster films continued:- 'Treasure Island' (Wallace Beery) 'The Iron Duke' (George Arliss), 'The Count of Monte Cristo' (Robert Donat), several double bills, 'The Merry Widow' (Maurice Chevalier and Jeanette McDonald). For 3 days 'Death at Broadcasting House' (Donald Wolfit's first film), 'Bulldog Drummond Hits Back' (Ronald Colman and Loretta Young), 'The Painted Veil (Garbo).

In August over a quarter of a million bricks had been laid by the Savoy (Newark) Ltd Company. Grand futuristic developments were envisaged. It was planned to seat 1450 patrons in comfort with curved rows and a screen set into the rear of the stage so that even in the front row there would be no distorted vision. Provision had been made in the plans for television. However overspending, carelessness and a lack of monetary control led to a situation whereby the possibility of completion looked increasingly in doubt.

Newark Cinemas purchased the unfinished cinema building. The Newark Directors of the Savoy Newark Ltd., Councillor T. J. Howitt and Mr K. Howitt, whose malt kilns provided the site for the Savoy and seats on the Savoy Board, joined the board of Newark Cinemas Ltd. The Savoy opened in its new colours on 30th January 1936. Several of the grand innovations were either abandoned or left covered over in the bowels and heights of the building. It was still an impressive building leaving the Palace the poor relation.

On 25th September the Palace was transformed into a court for a trial. The judge arrived at 7.30 p.m. to hear the four claimants with Counsel and a jury. However this was not a trial to penalise the claimants but to award a flitch of bacon to one of the 4 couples competing to be adjudged happiest couple in Newark. The qualification was that the couple should have lived happily for a year and a day.

As an innovtion to the Newark Carnival the Flitch trial filled not only the Cinema but the Cafe and the small games room (probably sitting on the billiards table). 1300 persons paid and many did not get in. *The Advertiser* carried the trial in full over 5 columns and the claimants laid bare their secrets under interrogation by the Counsel and the Judge. One of the personalities competing was Alan Menmuir, now managing director of the prosperous Blagg & Johnson. Such was the interrogation that couples were reluctant to volunteer in the following year.

The Theatre was closed for one day in November for an election meeting and from 25th to 27th November the Newark Amateur Dramatic Society presented 'And So To Bed' in aid of the Nurses and Hospital of Newark at 7.15. The price was 3/-, 2/- and 1/-. Miss Diana Berry with her Newark School of Dance presented a type of Pantomime with 'Jan of Windmill Land'. Prices were 2/4d, 1/10d and 1/2d.

With the Savoy being acquired surprisingly easily Newark Cinemas had to complete the building and plan for a 3 cinema capacity allocating to each cinema their future rôle. The Kinema was closed a good part of the year until returning in the Autumn with lower prices 1/-, 9d and 6d, now known locally by some as the 'bug hutch'.

5.   Operatic Society demand a stage

The unique Palace stage was in demand from the Amateur groups. In April came The Newark Orchestra and Operatic Society's production of 'The Mikado'. Prices were from 4/6d, 3/- and 2/3d. The receipts were £420 having had a total attendance of 4,000 over the week but still made a loss. During the Summer break The Newark District Ancient Order of Foresters annual Jubilee treat took place at Sconce Hills and the Palace.

The September Newark Carnival again presented the Flitch Trial at the Palace. Couples were reticent to undergo extensive interrogations. Three couples were found with difficulty but the fourth was Billy Merson and his partner Babs Valerie. They had come as the professional entertainers. Despite this difficulty the Palace was again packed and a good time was had by all. It didn't do Billy Merson any harm, one of his films appeared at the Palace a year later. The Police court furniture was borrowed by the committee for realism and returned undamaged. Tickets were 3/6d, 3/-, 2/- and 1/-. Receipts for the Flitch were £120 12s. 9d and expenses £59 2s. 6d.

On 30th October the Newark High School Speech day at the Palace was held. From Monday November 30 until Wednesday the Newark Amateur Dramatic Society presented '77 Dock Lane'. Prices were 3/-, 2/-, 1/- and 6d. The rest of the time in 1936 was taken up with good films while the Savoy provided the cream. This relegation continued through-out its future cinema life.

1937 opened with Mrs Diana Berry's pantomime 'Lollipopland' from the 11th to 13th January in aid of the National Children's Home and the Society for Prevention of Cruelty to Children at 7.15. Prices 3/-, 2/6d, 2/-, 1/6d and 1/2d. In January came the Chaplin film 'Modern Times'. On the 31st January The Edwinstowe Male Voice Choir and a prize band provided a Sunday concert. Prices 2/-, 1/6d, 1/- and 6d.

From 5th to 10th April the Newark Operatic Society presented 'Iolanthe'. Ticket prices were very expensive 6/- to 1/3d. On 15th September the Carnival Burlesque committee provided a St Anilands School Mock Annual Prize Giving. The 2 houses were packed (2500 customers). From the 18th November to 20th November The Newark Amateur Dramatic Society presented 'Tons of Money' in aid of the

District Nursing Association.

1938 opened with another production from the pupils of Newark School of Dance from 10-12th January called 'The Magic Key'. Prices were 3/6, 2/8d, 2/2d, 1/8d and 1/3d.

'The Gondoliers' was presented by the Newark Operatic Society at the Palace between the 21st and 26th February. Seat prices, which like the Newark School of Dance had risen, were reduced to 4/6 - 1/-. On Monday a seats offer was made, two seats for the price of one. 'The Gondoliers' was a virtual sell out. The Full House Board was displayed on Monday.

From 5th to 7th May came 'The Desert Song'. Not by the NAOS organisation. Mrs Ernest Randall mounted the production in aid of the Waifs and Strays Society. This new company of amateurs was a welcome addition to the live theatre devotees. It was billed as the 'most magnificent stage play ever seen in Newark. Prices were modest

Amongst the films 'Ebb Tide' claimed to be the first sea story to be filmed in colour. One of the better films was Paul Muni in 'The Good Earth' lasting 138 minutes.

By special request in August 'The Barretts of Wimpole Street' was repeated (Shearer, Laughton & March). 3/-, 2/- and 1/-. From the 6th to the 7th the Newarkandian Follies in aid of the Mayors Newark Hospital Appeal Fund and Newark Boys' Club. This entertainment in the programme apologised that

"owing to the international situation it was decided by the Committee to omit a very good but very tense and rather blood thirsty sketch."

The show produced a profit of £200. In November 'South Riding' came starring Ralph Richardson followed by 'A Star is Born', 'The Prisoner of Zenda' and John Hall and Dorothy Lamour in 'The Hurricane'.

As the war drew nearer 1939 continued the now familiar pattern of films and amateur live shows. As attendances were solidly good and Newark Cinemas Ltd had retained a monopoly of cinema entertainment in Newark there seemed no prospect of change, especially as the future seemed uncertain any innovations would now be made at the premier cinema the Savoy.

Live entertainment commenced with the Newark Amateur Operatic Society presenting 'The Yeoman of the Guard' from the 6th to 11th of

February 1939. Profits were in aid of the Newark Cripples Guild.

While the Palace showed 'The Girl of the Golden West' a second birthday week was celebrated at the Savoy. A different film every night plus a live band. In March the Savoy hosted an evening with Gypsy Petulengro with supporting Romany music and Anyeta The Dancer. I would imagine that this was a year in which astrology would be very popular. The Palace, the middle child, continued with films including 'The Lady Vanishes'.

From the 6th to the 8th March The Newark Amateur Dramatic Society presented 'Recipe for Murder'. This was followed by 'The Maid of the Mountains' another initiative by Mrs Ernest Randall in aid of the Waifs and Strays Society. Prices were modestly 3/-, 2/- and 1/- running from 24th to 29th April. Further films included Norma Shearer in 'Marie Antoinette' and Richard Greene in 'Submarine Patrol'.

On 2nd September war was declared and a National decree ordered all Cinemas to be closed.

Chapter 4

THE WAR AND POST WAR YEARS 1939-58

1.   A Call to Arms

On the 11th September 1939 the cinemas reopened with continuous showings from 2.30 p.m., Savoy only. From 6 p.m. the Palace and Kinema. All had to close at 10 p.m.

From the 2nd October for a week several films from America sponsored by the British Social Hygiene Council were shown. They covered 'social disease' 'Marriage Forbidden', women working after marriage, 'Men are such Fools', 'Accidents Will Happen' exposure of faked accidents. This film starred 'a recent discovery' Ronald Reagan! Monday was set aside 'for Ladies only'. Quite soon 7th October the Savoy reverted to a 6 p.m. opening time. The cinemas both began carrying the latest war news in picture. Typical military films showing at the cinemas were 27/10/1939 'Men with Wings' billed as 'the first aerial picture in technicolour'.

The enthusiasm of the Amateur Societies was undiminished. The Newark Amateur Dramatic Society presented on 15th December for 2 performances of 'For Goodness Sake' in aid of the Mayor's Comforts For The Troops fund at 2/-, 1/3, 1/-, 9d with 6d for troops.

With huge concentrations of the armed services in and around the town the cinemas had no troubles regarding attendances. Other venues were set up to provide morale boosting leisure time entertainment for the troops which included The Corn Exchange, The Town Hall, The Technical College and Northgate House which had also set up a canteen. The factory canteens were also in use. In 1941 Gracie Fields gave 2 concerts 'in a works canteen' and Northgate House. A celebrity concert was held at R&M's canteen in 1943 with Joan Hammond and Heddle Nash.

American films in colour were generally available but film copies were worked very hard and projection staff would find repair jobs increasing.

The Palace's first casualty of war was the cafeteria which was closed and cutlery stock and equipment transferred to the Savoy. It never reopened.

1939 ended with the British film 'Q Planes'. On week 13th January 1940 Monday to Wednesday it was 'Navy Secrets' with 'The Spy in Black' ending the week plus the latest war news. Later in February came 'Shipyard Sally' with Gracie Fields.

On 17th April the Newark Operatic Society presented a concert version for one night of 'H.M.S. Pinafore' charging 2/-, 1/6, 1/-. Troops in uniform half price 2 performances 6.15 and 8.30.

One might have thought the war situation was deteriorating because the Palace revealed 'Old Mother Riley Joins Up'. This film was supported by 'Battle over Norway' a documentary.

Secrecy was everywhere. Local inhabitants would have wandered around the town to reassure themselves that this report in the *Herald* did not refer to Newark.

'MIDLAND RAID BOMBS ON THEATRE'.

"Three of four incendary bombs had fallen on to the roof of the theatre starting small fires. While being dealt with the high explosive bomb shattered the glass works at the front of the house. The play continued and the audience remained calmly in their seats in the theatre until the raid was over."

During the war the Palace roof provided an excellent lookout view over the countryside and the projectionists climbed around inside the roof over the stage fire watching equipped with stirrup pump, fire axe and bucket of sand. The RAF presented the 'Spitfire Revue' at the Technical College . In December the Palace featured Arthur Askey in a film version of 'Charley's Aunt'.

At this time Newark Cinemas Adverts contained worthy wartime exhortations e.g. 'Remember go for it!' Christmas day the Palace was open from 6 p.m.. By March the slogans had changed to 'Lend to Defend', 'Bank for Tanks!', 'Keep it up', Keep it to yourself', 'Don't think of the Past', 'Look forward to the Future', 'We can take it', 'We have taken it, we can give it', 'We are hitting back', 'Stick together'. 'VVV'

Escapism featured in August with 'Down Argentine Way' with Don Ameche. After a longer slogan 'Weld yourselves together and don't rely on others for V', a halt was made.

Several procedures and adaptations had been made within the Palace occasioned by the war. A lantern in the roof was removed to aid access and provide an improved view over the area for the firewatchers.

Lighting was dimmed and any external windows covered with boarding to prevent the escape of light during the blackout. This was particularly important in the foyer area where an intermediate curtain between cinema entrance and the exits was erected. Performances could only begin when all patrons were seated.

Should the siren be sounded warning everyone of an impending air raid, then the manager would inform patrons should they wish to leave and seek the shelters or continue in their seats for the remainder of the performance. Ice creams or other refreshments were no longer available to sell. The upstairs dance room was used as sleeping quarters for the fire watchers.

In 1942 one second feature called 'Invasion' showed how an invasion would really happen in England. 'Everyone should see this picture'. 'March of Time' features included 20 minutes on 'The Battle of the Pacific' a complete story of the Far East situation. 'Victory over Darkness'. 'In the Rear of the Enemy' (the Russian front) which ran for 55 minutes.

2.   It'll Cost You More!

The increasing cost of the war was felt by the Cinemas from 18th May 1942 with an extra War Tax. Seat prices were increased to Circle 2/-, Stalls 1/3d and pit 10d. However audiences continued at capacity level. One reason was the extra monies earned by the hugely increased employment of women during the war.

During the summer the cinemas would close in turn for refurbishments. In 1943 the Palace closed from 14th June to 28th June. In one of these breaks the Palace was rewired and back in May 1941 a new screen 20ft 6in. by 15ft 6in. was fitted. The occasional slogan still appeared in the advertisements in 1943. It stated 'You'll never get rich - unless you save'. One main documentary film was 'Desert Victory' with the gallant eighth army. On 17th May 1943 further new War Taxes commenced. The circle was priced at 2/3d, Stalls 1/6d and Pit 1/-.

The invasion of 6th June was celebrated with a documentary showing all the preparations for D Day called 'The Eve of Invasion'.

The euphoria of the allied successes was embodied in the new documentary films such as 'Blasting the retreating Hun' tempered by the sudden arrival of the German V1 rockets; 'London's 80 day Ordeal' V1.

On Tuesday 8th of May 1945 came Victory over Europe (VE) Day and on 14th August 1945 came Victory over Japan (VJ) Day. In between came the 25th Anniversary of the Palace Theatre. This was celebrated on 28th September 1945 in the Savoy Cafe with a Silver Jubilee Lunch. But it was more than this. The Chairman Mr Ransom Harrison stated

"that they (Newark Cinemas) had been thinking how they could celebrate their anniversary which had been largely due to the patronage of Newark people. They decided to give something back - to Newark Hospital."

Mr Harrison said that

"although most of the company's revenue went to their partners, the Government and the film renters they decided to set aside three days takings for the Hospital."

The film chosen was 'Her Jungle Love' starring Ray Milland and Dorothy Lamour and filmed in technicolour. It ran from Monday to Wednesday 24th to 26th September 1945. This raised the sum of £279 15s. 4d. A further £75 and 1d was given by patrons in the form of a collection. A total of £354 15s. 5d. The directors decided that this was insufficient and they resolved that the sum should be £1000 to endow a bed. The cheque of £354 was therefore handed over as a first instalment. Mr Blatherwick Chairman of the hospital board said that

"despite his receiving many hundreds of cheques very few had been received with greater pleasure than this one. It was a fine gift and a generous gift."

Before coming to the meeting he had been sitting with Mr Cann in hospital and knew how deeply he felt being absent from that celebration. Mr Cann, who became manager of the Kinema from 1920 and added the Palace to his duties on the resignation of Mr Armstrong in 1933 had managed both throughout the war. A shareholder in Newark Cinemas and owner of a wallpaper shop in Cartergate, he was really the last of the original senior staff. Only Mr Priestly remained. Classified as day man in the wages sheet he was a man of many parts who began his Newark career at the Kinema, just prior to its opening in 1913.

The Herald commented that Newark was inadequately served regarding live theatre.

During the war Blagg & Johnson had made 2¼ million pressings weighing over 8700 tons which were used for Bailey & Pontoon bridges, amphibious vehicles, travelling work shops and for waterproofing tanks for D Day beaches.

In 1946 and 1947 the Palace continued showing a good selection of

The Palace Theatre Staff; Back Row L to R : Pat Priestly, Dick . . . , Oliver Cousins, Jack . . . , Cyril Stevenette. Front Row to R : Mrs Kirk Mary King, Oliver . . . . / . . . . /, Judy Brown and Mary Homes.

The Palace Theatre Staff c. 1950.

films though not new 'The Adventures of Robin Hood' and 'Henry VIII and his Wives'.

Early in 1947 the Newark Operatic Society reformed after a lapse of seven years. The first post war production was to be 'The Gondoliers'. Mr George Bennett explained that

> "the principal difficulty about doing a show is that we have nowhere to produce it. Before the war we used the Palace, but now we have been told that we cannot have either the Palace or the Kinema. Certainly in Newark there is now nowhere we could put on a show on our pre war scale. Even a cramped show will be something and we will have restarted our activities."

The Ideal Cinema Southwell put on a full scale live pantomime with a professional company.

In 1948 some programmes were very weak e.g. William Boyd in 'Borderland' with full supporting programmes and 'Roy Rogers, 'Home in Oklahoma'. Then came a 2¼ hour full length technicolour film of the London 1948 Olympics.

During 1949 while films continued at the Palace, the Savoy in February provided Sonja and Partner, a thought transference live act, followed in July by a variety show starring Bill Kerr. It drew capacity audiences for each of the 2 houses. Was this the death knell for live theatre at the Palace!

The Herald in May 1949 carried an article of Newark Theatres from the past and the author G. A. Barnes states

> "No longer are we privileged to see the great actors and actresses unless we travel to neighbouring cities. We should express our sincere gratitude and give the strongest possible support to those groups of Newark Amateurs who give their time and talents in the production of dramatic and musical entertainments in this town. It would seem that celluloid has overcome the arts of the human."

In April 1950 Mr Frank Lacey Chief Projectionist at Newark Cinemas for 27 years retired and was presented with 2 fireside chairs by Mr J. Pollard Joint Managing Director Newark Cinemas Ltd. He also announced new appointments. Mr H. L. Perkin would be General Manager of Newark Cinemas following on from Mr Jack Cann and Mr Oliver Cousins would be manager of the Palace.

Mr Pollard seemed to worry about the future in his speech. Certain changes are taking place in the entertainment business generally. Television was looming largely on the horizon. He had been in London recently and had seen a picture televised as large as a cinema screen quite clearly and free from interference.

In 1952 the last link with the past went with 'Pat' Priestley who retired at 65. Mostly resplendant in his fine Commissionnaire's uniform he had also been stage manager for live stage productions but generally a man of the cinema age.

3.   A Change in Management

The Palace closed for 2 weeks in the summer. The Board of Newark Cinemas Ltd had grown old and ready for retirement in a changing scene. All their glories were in the past. A huge amount of money was needed to restore the stage equipment if live entertainment was ever to return to the Palace. Doubtless, being locally respected citizens with benevolent intentions, they would continually have been nudged repeatedly by those wishing for a theatre and live entertainment. This was not really economically viable. At the conclusion of the War the fire regulations were enforced. I have been told of a bonfire of old scenery, back cloths and flats outside the Palace. None of which was fireproof. The equipment was generally outdated and obsolescent. No blame can be attached to Newark Cinemas Ltd for the existing situation but Newark needed new blood.

On 15th November 1952 Star Cinemas London Ltd made an offer for the company Newark Cinemas Ltd to acquire the whole of the £70,000 £1 ordinary shares at £1.75 per share. The Directors of Newark Cinemas Ltd and the three Newark Cinemas became part of the Star circuit from the 1st January 1953.

The change in ownership was mutually beneficial to both Companies and to the people of Newark. The Star Cinemas organisation had begun in 1931 when Walter Eckart a London based toy importer bought the New Star cinema in Castleford Yorkshire for £7,000. By 1939 he had 16 cinemas and by 1953 a chain of over 100 cinemas. By this time sons Rodney and Derek had joined this expansionist, close, family business. The acquisition of a prestige cinema, a Theatre with large excellent stage which had a scarcity value in the group and a normal town cinema was another step towards an ever growing national power base. It was reckoned to be one of the best managed groups within the Industry.

1953 was a crossroads year. Cinema attendances had declined by over a quarter in the decade 1946 (£1635 million attendances) 1956 (£1182 million attendances). Newark Cinemas traditional thrifty relaxed local and quite paternalistic saw the trend as disturbing. Star Cinemas alias The Eckhart family regarded the figures not only a chance to acquire futher cinemas but a temporary depression that would be reversed when the right remedies were applied. Mr Eckart stated in his policy remarks that

> "we have every confidence in the future of our industry and hope that the support of the Newark people will be such that eventually the town will be recognised as a leading centre of entertainment offering facilities in keeping with the status of one of the larger towns in the area."

4.   Pantomime Returns

Star Cinemas had studied the local entertainment scene and began immediately taking steps to revitalise their latest acquisitions. Mr Eckart called together his suppliers and technical experts who descended upon the Palace and with Palace management and staff worked night and day over the Christmas period to clean, renovate and refurbish the theatre in order to present a live pantomime 'Mother Goose' on stage from the fifth to the tenth of January 1953. One performance at 7 p.m. per night Monday to Friday and three performances on Saturday at 2.30, 5.30 and 8 p.m. Admission prices were Dress Circle and Orchestra Stalls 5/-, Children 3/6d, Balcony and Stalls 4/-, Children 3/-, Pit Stalls 3/-, Children 2/-.

'The Spectacular All Star Pantomime' starred Frankie Murray and Billie Ponds. However perhaps two lesser featured players are probably remembered best, Don Arrol the comedian and Jerry Allen the organist who provided the pantomime's accompaniment. Speciality acts were provided by Itrebors Fifteen Wonder Pigeons, Joseph Kirby's World Famous Flying Ballet and the Gooseland Girls and full London Company.

The Pantomime company was engaged by Star Cinemas to tour all their theatres. So the furtherance of pantomimes depended upon their success throughout the Group and not just the success in Newark. However 'Newark's Pantomime Mother Goose packs Palace' was the headline in the *Herald*. 'Nearly nine thousand people will have seen the Pantomime when it closes a successful week tonight'. There was a full house on Monday evening and heavy bookings were repeated on every other evening.

I was told that during the overnight working necessary to transform the neglected stage, backstage and lighting system over the Xmas period one of the huge steel 18 foot towers carrying the giant loudspeakers suddenly moved. It is a credit to the professionalism of the staff that they preferred to face the supernatural rather than disappoint Star Cinemas patrons.

Although the Palace stage was again in action the period of neglect, post war safety regulations and obsolescence had created a situation whereby to restore the stage to its former glories instead of desperate make do and mend compromises would be very costly. Mr Eckart was fully aware of the situation and addressed the lack of a venue for Newark's Amateur Dramatic and Operatic Societies.

"If Newark's Palace Theatre is equipped for live stage shows, local societies will be welcome to use it. A decision on the future of the Palace will be forthcoming in due course. The wishes of the public will be borne in mind but that is tied up with what the local Authority will let us do. Notts C.C. will insist that a great deal of work must be effected to the stage before there can be regular presentations of live shows and the sum involved is such that we have to decide whether or not such large expenditure is justifiable. We would not turn the Palace into a full time live theatre because we are cinema people."

Meanwhile several innovations had been put into operation by Star Cinemas which did not affect the Palace. A young citizens club began with a club magazine (childrens club activities everywhere) and of course the childrens Saturday matinee at the Savoy.

On the opening night of the Savoy after refurbishment a packed audience had the pleasure of seeing 'Starlight on Newark' a 30 minute film made by the Star Cinemas Film unit production 'starring You the people of Newark'. The film the Company's own camera men shot in the town. Patrons were also able to view and appreciate the many improvements which 'Star' have effected in the foyer and theatre for their comfort.

Star also promised

"No matter how much or how little a person may pay for a seat in a cinema that person is entitled to comfort, clean and hygenic surroundings, a clear picture, good sound and finally the best possible programme available."

One change at the Palace also highlighted the change of status of the manager. His downstairs office was restored to use as a tenanted shop while he occupied the small upstairs room known as Miss Ralph's room.

The next live show at the Palace was not until 11th January 1954 when 'Jack and the Beanstalk' was presented for a week.

"A grand family laughter pantomime with a big star cast of favourites and specialities. A feast of fun for everyone plus Britain's most popular organist Robbie and his £2000 organ. Twelve glorious scenes."

Edna Dean was principal boy and Joe Walmer as Simon. Kirby's Flying Ballet returned and good business was done. Robbies portable organ was very versatile and was capable, when dismantled, of being stored in his van. However it was felt that on the final evening after all had been packed that an outside location for the organ was a bit risky and the organ itself should be stored within the Palace. Making an early start next morning Robbie did not realise until he arrived at his next destination that the organ was still at the Palace. That evening he played a Grand Piano!

In June 1953 Star Cinemas had requested that the Council should discuss Sunday Cinema opening in Newark. By the 29th March 1954 The Town Council approved by 14 votes to 5 with 2 abstentions a formal resolution bringing into operation Section One of the Entertainments Act of 1932. The decision now rested with the electorate meeting to be held 21st April 1954 at 7 p.m. in the Town Hall. Star Cinemas had organised a petition of 5,100 signatures advocating Sunday Cinema opening plus, 257 signatures from the armed forces in the locality. However despite the measures taken to rouse support from their patrons the Lords Day observance society and the Newark ministers expressed opposition.

On the 14th April the cinema advertisements urged 'Sunday Cinemas Don't Forget the Public Meeting' and on 21st April 'You have signed the petition NOW make sure you attend the meeting tonight'.

Usually these meeting were informal however Newark insisted on the letter of the law. Volunteer corporation workers manned the barrier beyond which only persons on the electoral roll were allowed to pass. So although the employees of Star Cinemas attended en masse most of the staff were either under age or lived outside the borough. Even the highly important Circuit Manager of Star Cinems Mr A. J. Brown who had travelled from Sheffield to speak was surprised to find himself excluded. He remarked that this was the first time this had ever happened to him. However on a vote of 133 to 40 Sunday Cinemas were accepted. The final appeal was to be allowed if objections were received within four days. However as no further objections were made Sunday Cinemas became a fact.

The first Sunday films were at the Palace on the 18th July. The films chosen were Dick Powell in 'Rogues Regiment' and Robert Stack in 'Badlands of Dakota'. The show was continuous from 5.30 until 9.45. No great films were shown on a Sunday. Distributors had rules that one day engagements should be several years old. But despite this Sunday attendances were usually most popular.

For the week 1st to 6th November the Palace hosted a 'Spectacular Skating Extravaganza' 'Cinderella on Ice' on Real Ice on the stage. The large circular tank with a waterproof stage cloth beneath was filled with ice by means of a compressor which was placed in the open passage between the engine house and the opposite back entrance of the Palace. With a packed warm theatre it had to work extremely hard to maintain the real ice. Several doors had to be left ajar to accommodate numerous cables. The show was a full pantomime with eight scenes and the following specialities: Ice Cyclist, International Pair Skating Stars Peter Perks and Janette, Ballet on Ice, Daisy the Cow, The Famous flashing blades of the Ladies of the Ice Skating Ballet and real ponies. Vic Templar starred and Robbie on his £2000 Hammond Organ accompanied.

This pantomime on ice was followed by the conventional pantomime from 10th January 1955 for a week. 'Robinson Crusoe' starred Eileen May in the title role. There were twelve spectacular scenes. Admission prices were from 5/6 to 3/6 with concessions for children and OAPs. Robbie again accompanied.

5.   Bring Back the Musical

In February 1955 The Newark Amateur Operatic Society announced that the first amateur show at the Palace since the first year of the war was to be 'The Quaker Girl'. It was to be one of the most ambitious shows ever attempted by the Society. To be staged from the 18th to 24th April.

The three hour show with a cast of 100 and at a cost of £800 was bold and the wide open spaces of the Palace stage after 'the restrictions of the technical college' provided a backdrop to the Society's biggest achievement in 20 years.

The £800 expenses bill was already covered by bookings received before Monday's first performance. These alone accounted for twice as many seats as could have been sold at the technical college, if every performance for a week had played to capacity audiences.

"It is not only the stage that is more roomy at the Palace, the weeks show provides places for a total audience of about 6,000 compared with 2,000 at the college. The large stage enables the Society to use standard scenery instead of having to construct its own portable sets. Backstage space enables producer George Bennett to providee entrances and exits, for the large chorus, and 52 juvenile dancers. This show could not have been presented at all on the limited Technical College stage. The only problem appears to be that 'the wide open spaces' of the auditorium made it appear that the cast were miming their parts so far as the back of the house audience is concerned'. It is perhaps a pity that theatrical tradition places the orchestra - well balanced and adequately drilled in itself - slap between the singers and the audience."

On the 14th May the Palace was given the Young Citizens Matinee Club and in June Cinemascope arrived at the Palace with 'Sitting Bull' and '20,000 Leagues Under the Sea' being the most spectacular presentations. The expense of the new innovations might have been a contributory factor to the decision in March 1956 not to renew the Theatre Licence:

"For the first time in its 35 years' existence Newark Palace Cinema is no longer fully licensed as a theatre. No application has been made for a renewal of the theatre license this year and consequently it has lapsed. But Newark Amateur Operatic Society will still be able to stage shows there. Continuing as a Cinema the Palace will be able to obtain up to two occasional theatre licenses yearly each covering a week of live entertainment. The change means that the Palace is no longer a theatre."

Mr Derek Eckart said that:

"We have given up the permanent stage licence because to have maintained it we should have had to do a tremendous amount of alterations. That is why there is no pantomime in Newark this year. It is a pity really because we thought Newark seemed to appreciate live entertainment.

The tremendous structural alterations that would be necessary to meet the licensing authorities modern requirements, the owners consider, are unjustified for at most a few weeks stage entertainment each year. The cost would also have been substantial."

The next live production at the Palace was the spectacular production of 'Rose Marie' by the Newark Amateur Operatic Society between the

16th and 23rd April 1956. This production it could be said had taken 16 years to emerge upon the stage. Originally it began rehearsals in the period of the 'phony war'. But 'the beginning in earnest' of Britains lone struggle for survival cut short the production. It never reached the stage. During the last few months the society had again been rehearsing - and this time 'the show goes on'. Ironically the production was the most lavish ever staged by the Society in stark contrast to the austerity conditions in 1940. The cost of production exceeded £1000 but was practically a complete sell out before the first night.

The production was superb. All the minor problems encountered with the Quaker Girl had been eliminated. The microphones set at footlight level produced a perfect sound reproduction. In fact this was a production on the same scale as the twenties London productions. A temporary taste of caviar for a hungry populace which yearned for a diet of live entertainment.

The orchestra with Elsie Pullant who has been the indefatigable accompaniest throughout the long rehearsals, were professional. The dress rehearsal was therefore the first coming together for chorus, principals and orchestra. It could not have been easy.

At this time advertisements appeared in the local papers for live entertainments at Nottingham and Lincoln.

In December Star Cinemas held the company's silver jubilee prizegiving at the Savoy Newark.

> "It was a compliment to Newark that this celebration took place here when the Star chain consisted of 116 houses up and down the country. Managers from all parts travelled to Newark."

It was a unique occasion for Newark because Mr Walter Eckart the Managing Director of Star Cinemas gave a frank and illuminating address on the problems of cinema management at a critical time for the cinema industry.

It was a company which believed that efficient realistic management would prevail against reductions in attendances. The 1956 figure of annual attendance £1,182 millions seemed low but in 1977 annual attendances were only 103 millions. Thus in these years more than 90% of the cinema audience had disappeared. Mr Walter Eckart alluded to 'a time of severe test' and addressed the problems.

He said that:

"The Public have developed an apathy towards the cinemas from which they were only occasionally shaken by the offering of an outstanding winner either a really great film or one with a gimmick. He declared that the new super length films may have marked the beginning of a new era of once nightly shows"

quoting 'War and Peace' and 'The Ten Commandments'.

Mr Eckart did not accept that television was the prime reason for apathy but the cinema trade

"For too long has the mediocre been foisted on the public: for too long has the independant producer taken advantage of the shortage of product, without regard for quality Films had been turned out quickly, to cash in on a waiting market."

He could forecast that

"some of his cinemas would close to avoid showing some of the tripe they are forced to screen."

'Whatever happens (comments Chiel in the Advertiser) it is evident that the films brought to Newark will be carefully watched by Mr Eckart and his colleagues. Mr Eckart had pertinent remarks regarding 'ancillary sales' of ice cream, minerals, sweets and cigarettes. He stated that

"they are so important that without them a third of the Star Cinema showings would reveal a loss. Films are being shown in some of our cinemas only to create a ready market for our sales."

'It is evident that the cinema business is one which requires careful and diligent management (says Chiel). With this in mind Star Cinemas had spent £278,000 during the past year in re-equipping and modernising cinemas, and in organising competitions to bring out the best in managers. The result is that men in charge have to be on their toes. They are in competition with managers in neighbouring towns. They have to be watchful, alert and enterprising. The 'end product' is the prize for efficiency. Thus the raison d étrè of the prizegiving ceremony. For instance prizes went to Newark managers for cleanliness and efficiency, publicity, good citizenship promotion, public relations effort, best kept projection boxes, kiosk sales and civic cooperation. This means that managers must be striving all the time to give the best service and in that way the public should benefit.

In 1957 the local papers were giving previews and reviews of live entertainments in Lincoln and Nottingham. The Palace was exploring continental films as in the nineteen twenties but not for such altruistic reasons. Although 'The Fiends' was a superb chiller and Brigitte Bardot's film 'The Light Across the Street' had merit as well as an erotic storyline, later films were more for the dirty raincoat brigade.

Between the 8th and 13th April the Newark AmateurOperatic Society presented 'A Country Girl'. One different type of theatregoing emerged.

"A handful of men will put on their oldest gardening clothes every night and go to the theatre. They have volunteered to help backstage at the Palace Cinema where a live show is to be staged for the first time for a year. Newark Amateur Operatic Society is experimenting this year by having amateur stagehands. In a few hours they will have to learn how to move towering stage flats quickly and quietly. Until late Sunday evening the Palace will be a cinema. The change to a theatre will take place during the night and on Monday is a tremendous undertaking. Biggest task is moving the widescreen and the speaker. Most tedious job is sticking numbers on to each of the 1113 seats. "

'A Country Girl' was a smooth swinging production and a great success. However with expenditure of £1114 and income of £1072 Chiel commented that

"the figures would deter professional management. The public has the advantage of seeing a live show, which is becoming a rarity in the town, and should contribute all possible support."

The Newark Young Citizens matinee club was thriving with 2 performances at 10 a.m. and 2 p.m. Mr Hughes the Palace manager received a commendation from the Kinematograph weekly for public relations with childrens matinees.

The evening performances presented 'Garden of Eden' (the American Sunbathing Society) and 'Female Jungle'. Mr Hughes had produced a Skiffle group at the children's matinee with the children singing to the skiffle accompaniment. In previous weeks the children held community singing sessions. The advertisement read 'All pals at The Palace'.

One Sunday show in 1957 presented 'White Zombie' (Bella Lugosi) and 'Flying Serpent' (George Zucco). Both pre war.

In April the Newark Amateur Operatic Society presented 'White Horse Inn' for the week.

In August a different entertainment was a contest by the Newark and District Physical Culture Show who gave an all star show and competition.

Chapter 5

SURVIVAL IN A CHANGING WORLD 1958-72

1.   Rock and Roll

In 1958 cinema presentations continued. The first innovation occurred in March when the Palace held a Skiffle Group Contest. This was followed by several films based upon the new popular music of rock and roll such as 'The Six Five Special', 'The Duke Wore Jeans' (Tommy Steele), 'Jailhouse Rock' (Elvis Presley), 'The Golden Disc' (Terry Dene). This was a build up heralding a different type of live entertainment.

During this period the Newark Star Junior Club was run by the inimitable Vina Cooke, with Arts and Craft classes in modelling and drawing. One of her successes was the colourful Easter Bonnets Display, which attracted thirty entrants. The children paraded across the stage, to be judged by Savoy restaurant manageress Miss M. Golland and Vina Cooke.

On Thursday 18th September Star Cinemas had enjoyed a variety show for one evening. Admission prices were Dress Circle and Orchestra Stalls 6/-, Centre Stalls 5/- and Rear Stalls 4/-. It starred Ray Ellington and his Quartet, probably most famous for his musical interludes and bit part actor in 'The Goon Show', Russ Hamilton who wrote 'Puff the Magic Dragon' and "the new teenage singing sensation Val Masters".

A visit to the show gave those buying programmes the chance for a weekend at Morecambe for the Illuminations. The lucky number printed on the programme as drawn during the performance entitled one person to a free weekend.

The show visited the theatres controlled by Star Cinemas. They were The Majestic Derby, Regal Cinema Worksop, Pavilion Cinema Scunthorpe, Empire Wombwell, Empire Cinema Shirebrook, Crescent Cinema Pontefract and of course the Palace.

From this presentation came not only a pantomime for Newark but visits from several chart topping stars. The Star organisation with its pool of trainee managers and anyone available in the locality was used not only in publicity but crowd supervision and protection of the artistes.

On Wednesday 19th November 1958 Marty Wilde, the John Barry Seven and Nancy Whiskey entertained the local pop generation. On the 22nd December the children of the Newark Young Citizens Club were given a free party with games and films provided they had obtained an admission ticket from Uncle Mac.

The sad news was that Newark's oldest Cinema, re-named The Ritz by Star Cinemas, formerly The Kinema but popularly known by the locals as the bug-hutch, was closed at the the end of April, a victim of the downturn in Cinema viewing, taxes and Walter Eckarts refusal to screen inferior films.

The first advertisements for the pantomime 'Cinderella' added the condition 'Licence applied for'. The Licence was obtained and for the week 12th January to 18th January Newark had its pantomime 'Cinderella' with Jimmy Slater, Leslie Gunby and Conchita Dawn.

Following the pantomime came the visit of probably Britains Greatest pop star, Cliff Richard. On Thursday 22nd January supported by Wee Willie Harris, The Bachelors and Tony Crombie and his Rockets, Kerry Martin and the Oomph girls of the 6.5 Special radio show. Cliff Richard drove the audience wild. An account of the visit was given by the *Newark Advertiser:-*

"Cliff Richard the idol of teenagers throughout the country was put in cold storage. Making his escape from the screaming teenagers he left the stage door in an ice cream van driven by Derek Priestley, stage manager.

Whilst the current teenage star was making his last curtain call the small blue and white van reversed up to the stage door with rear doors open. Wee Willie Harris held the attention of the audience while Richard slipped offstage into a coat held by his manager and straight into the waiting van.

From the first opening of the curtains the 1,100 strong audience had screamed their way through a programme of special appeal to teenagers. They screamed and hardly a sound of the music penetrated a wall of frantic female exhibitionism. Typical of the enthusiasm was a girl perched on the edge of her seat on the front row. Throughout the show she bounced excitedly clapping in time with the music. Probably she could hear on the front row. And then Cliff Richard appeared. The girl went hysterical. With each wiggle she ecstatically reached up with both hands towards him. Even after the timely disappearance of the star the crowds waited. Only 20 or so of the audience saw him beat a hasty retreat to his hotel but they stayed on. Still inside was Harris. It was 11 o'clock before he managed to get clear in the same Morris 1000 that had helped the escape of Marty Wilde at the last one night stand held at the theatre.

On Friday morning the doors at the main entrance to the theatre were minus one

102

Vina Cooke presenting Cliff Richard with a doll she had made for the rock singer. Soon afterwards he achieved fame with the song, "Living Doll".

ornate handle. It had been wrenched off by the crush outside. The van which made Richard's escape possible was later discovered covered with messages written in lipstick."

We must praise the reporter who although most bemused by this new phenomena has documented the occasion for posterity.

The wave of euphoria continued on Thursday 26th February with a one night stand of 'The King Brothers', Russ Conway, The John Barry Seven, Don Rennie and The Avon Sisters. A galaxy of disc stars that night was eagerly awaited'. "Two Nottingham girls spent three and a half hours in Newark on Thursday afternoon waiting to see the King Brothers. Their reward was an autograph and a snatch of conversation with the three singing brothers they have followed around the country. On Thursday evening the girls had a further reward when they were in the 1,100 strong audience. And it was a reward. The programme presented by Star Cinemas was good and of wider appeal than the previous one night stands at the theatre which have tended to appeal almost entirely to the teenage rock enthusiasts".

The next one night stand was on Wednesday 18th March with stars Jill Day, Johnny Duncan and his Blue Grass Boys, Billy Fury and Vince Taylor and his playboys. Prices for 1959 were always 6/6d, 5/6d and 4/6d.

On the 16th April Marty Wilde made a return visit to Newark Palace along with his wildcats, Malcolm Vaughan and Kenneth Earle, Cuddley Dudley and the Carson twins. When asked by the reporter had he some secret regard for Newark in view of his early return visit to the Palace. Marty was agog, he had not realised that he had ever visited Newark before.

The Newark Amateur Operatic Society returned from 20-26th April with 'The Gondoliers'. On Sunday 14th June on stage came Len and Lyn Paule direct from recent variety successes. This was variety combined with a film. In July came the Summer Beat Wave with Billy Fury who gallantly offered a lift home to a Lincoln girl when she had dallied beyond the last bus home. Arriving in Lincoln where an unforgettable night ended with the appearance of the girl's father, a swift kiss and a fast getaway by the star leaving the house gate demolished.

These pop shows were one way in which Star Cinemas compensated for the lower income from films due to the continual decline in attendances. Another experiment came on Friday evening 11th September. Matt Lewis promotions presented an evening of professional free style wrestling. Prices were ringside 8/6d to 4/6d Circle 7/6d. The main event was the light heavyweight champion of Germany Hans Streiger (Dortmund) against Mighty Elmo Foy (Bolton) Amateur Heavyweight Champion of the World. This was preceded by 3 other contests. Undoubtedly the question was where was the ring?

For each promotion the ring was secured from the edge of the stage to the row of seating on a level with the stage. Any loss of seating was made up by extensive seating on the stage. Huge support beams took the strain of the contests. One cynic alleged that a certain amount of choreography went on and perhaps one corner was not as secure as the other three and coincidentally much action occurred in this corner especially by heavyweights. Should this escalate coincidentally by supportive seconds hanging onto the ring to inform the referee of injustices to their fighters. And should the referee arrive into the embattled area and several spectators wish to counsel the referee then there would be a fair chance that the corner would collapse and please the expectant audience. Further regular wrestling events came in October and November.

1960 opened with a pantomime from the 18th to 24th January. 'Red Riding Hood' was billed as 'carefree entertainment for the whole family'. 'The most lavish glittering pantomime ever presented in Newark'. In March a further stage show came starring Lance Fortune, Wee Willie Harris, Edna Savage and the Fleerakkers. On the 4th to 9th April The Newark Amateur Operatic Society presented 'The Merry Widow'. At the end of June a prestige film 'The Nuns Story' came to the Palace for nine days.

From the 17th to 30th July the Palace closed for the holiday season. For the Kinema's last years it often had a holiday closure. Then for several months before it closed some of the seating disappeared. However during the summer attendances were down and films of quality more difficult to obtain. There seemed also several gaps in the autumn of newspaper advertisements for the Palace.

2.   All Star Wrestling

In 1961 the future of the Cinema industry looked bleak. Star group cinemas had virtually ceased to expand its ownership of cinemas. By the late fifties having a chain of 120 which was only a few more than when the three Newark cinemas were acquired. However several cinemas were closed and sold including the Kinema/Ritz.

Derek Eckart admitted in 1971 that

"when competition from television began to bite the change in tastes could have been disasterous for Star. We were sitting on a lot of halls quite a few of which were ailing."

Star diversified into Silver Blades Ice Rinks. However its salvation was as Rodney Eckart put it

"Out of heaven came the 1960 Gaming Act which triggered off the Bingo Boom. Overnight the profits were there."

This was speaking retrospectively in fact it took time to experiment and gauge the extent and duration of the Bingo phenomenan.

The Palace Pantomime was no more. Matt Lewis promoters and Wrestling had gone and apparently the pop one night stands had also gone.

Professional Wrestling was re-introduced. Obviously popular in the last year but now promoted by a top promoter Relwyskow and Green Promotions Ltd. who presented top names. Billy Two Rivers, the only full blooded Red Indian wrestler appearing in Great Britain, appeared on the first bill on 8th February 1961 at 7.30 p.m. Prices of admission were 10/6d to 3/6. All seats bookable. The advertisement stated:

"Relwyskow and Green are members of joint promotions Ltd exclusive contractors to I.T.V. for wrestling. No other body presents wrestling on I.T.V. and only with Relwyskow and Green will Newark fans see the I.T.V. stars in their home town."

This was a commercial attack upon the established venue at the Corn Exchange. Although they could not match the quality of the Palace such names as Leon Arras (Now actor Brian Glover) appeared.

They also cunningly presented their promotions the evening before the Palace promotion. It was however a hopeless struggle against promotions that boasted that on its 4th March promotion part of the sensational All Star programme would be televised by ABC Television. Was it the Mike Marino v Jose Arroyo bout or the Inca Pernana v Mick McManus bout? It appears that Joint Promotions Ltd were also Alliance

106

Europeane de lutt de Combat.

Bookings were always taken at the Savoy. The Palace was only open during the evening. It had no manager and a skeleton evening staff. However no seats had disappeared!

The situation was poor for the Palace it looked seedy, dilapidated and was not paying its way. Audiences were poor, as low as single figures some evenings. It was given the poorer films because a good film at the Palace always did worse than at the Savoy because of the less attractive surroundings.

The skeleton staff consisted of one projectionist full time, one cashier evenings, one usherette upstairs, one usherette downstairs, a sales girl in the kiosk partly commision based, a casual visit occasionally by the Savoy manager and a trainee projectionist, who became redundant when automatic projection arrived.

All administration was done from the Savoy. Takings for the evening were taken to the Savoy each evening. Often during staff shortages the cashier would be used for both cinemas. The backstage was usually ignored between visits of NAOS. Sundays were well attended, requiring a couple of well built male attendants in case of trouble.

The all star wrestling continued on the 29th March with Tommy Mann and Bert Royal, 12th April with John Allan, Alan Dennison and Masambula and 10th May Bert Royal, John Allan and Ray St Clair (admissions 6/-, 4/6 and 3/-).

The wide screen at this time was showing 'The King and I', 'South Pacific' and 'Dam on the Yellow River.

An International Wrestling bill with Les Kellet and Ben Youssef Ayoub was scheduled but not held owing to Ben Youssef being unable to attend. The promotors said that they would not put on a substitute bill. Their reputation would suffer and so the promotion was cancelled. The Palace again closed for the annual holidays and re-opened in August.

At this time distributors had obtained classic films which if sponsored by local organisations could be shown. The Newark Music Club presented a showing of 'Don Giovanni' as one example.

All Star wrestling recommenced on Saturday 30th September 1961. Continued on 14th October, 11th November and 9th December, with such wrestlers as Ian Campbell, Jim Breaks, Les Kellett, Tommy Mann and Alan Dennison. This December promotion seems to have been the final wrestling promotion. Films included two originally 3D films now shown flat 'House of Wax' and 'Charge at Feather River'.

3.   Full Time Bingo

On 29th November the *Newark Advertiser* carried an advertisement proclaiming in large letters

"'Its Here... At Last' 'The Biggest Value for money Bingo ever'. From 3rd December 1961 every Sunday at 2.45 p.m. Doors open 1.45 p.m. 'Let Bingo help to fill your CHRISTMAS STOCKING'."

The Star Super no limit Bingo Club had arrived.

This introductory time slot disturbed nothing, whilst providing extra use and generating income to the Palace. It was such a great success that it was compelled to be a 'Members only'. Bingo Club.

All available staff were utilized in posting application forms in every letter box in Newark while an advert in the *Advertiser* on 18th December stated

"Due to overwhelming public demand admission is restricted to "members only", who must register 24 hours before using the clubs premises.

So the world of '2 little ducks', 'legs 11', 'was she worth it' was to resound throughout the Palace for the next decade.

However innovation and publicity was still employed to create a cinema audience. When 'The Pit and the Pendulum' came the challenge was made. '£10,000 if you die of fright'. 'The first person who dies of fright watching the film is insured for £10,000'. Presumably the audience had strong hearts because no claim was made. The 1962 films included a large portion of erotica:- 'Sun Lovers Paradise', 'Pamela Green', 'Naked As Nature Intended', 'Nudes of the World', House of Sun' and 'The Fruit is Ripe'.

In April the Newark Amateur Operatic Society presented 'Carousel'. But what of the vital Sunday afternoon rehearsal? This went ahead while the Bingo club enlivened the Savoy for the afternoon, while the Sunday film at the Palace was cancelled.

From the 19th October 1962 Bingo took over on Friday nights. Within another seven weeks Bingo included every Thursday and

Monday. However while Friday was exclusively Bingo, Monday and Thursday consisted of 'Cine-Bingo'.

"The General public and members admitted to film performances. The latest sensation. The film commenced at 6.30 p.m. and members only can remain to play Bingo from 8.30. After the Bingo New Thrilling Legalite roulette direct from the Continent. Enjoy a full evenings entertainment for only 2/6d stalls and 3/3d circle.

Roulette and the Casino atmosphere did not endear themselves to Newark and were soon dropped.

For those people who have never played Bingo I will attempt an explanation. Cards are purchased containing 15 random numbers from 1 to 90. A caller reads out a selection of numbers. The sole idea is to win money. The only skill is to cross off numbers on the cards you have purchased, then luck and the ability to notice that your card has been completely crossed off before the next number is called plus the ability to shout at that instant 'House', 'Here' or any other acceptable call. The game is then stopped for verification. If correct the money is paid to the winner. If incorrect a 'bogey' is called and the game continues. The tension as all players approach a full card is electric. Then the next game commences.

Usually every seat was full. So staffing was uniform. The most important official was the caller who sat on the stage behind a machine ejecting coloured balls containing random numbers which were relayed to the audience by the caller's microphone. There were several checkers throughout the hall awaiting a call of house, locating that call and checking off that card with the official caller. There were several cashiers selling game books on entering the hall and a lighting engineer.

The only alteration to cinema was much heightened lighting as dim cinema lighting would make it impossible to read the cards.

By July 1963 'The Palace Casino' held four sessions in the evenings, Thursday, Friday, Saturday and Monday with a Sunday afternoon session. This frequency caused problems with the film distributors who usually insisted that a cinema must have at least 4 days each week to receive films. This was why the marriage of convenience of Cine-Bingo was commenced.

At this time the Corn Exchange hosted The Sunshine Bingo Club. It usually held sessions on those evenings that the Palace showed films. The childrens matinees continued. The Newark Operatic soldiered on

109

trying to produce musical comedy excellence in spite of being sand-wiched in between the ever increasing bingo sessions and the theatre's film commitments, on an ever deteriorating stage area. I was told that rot was evident at one point on the stage.

Of course as Christmas approached Bingo sessions saturated the theatre. 'Sunday, Monday, Tuesday, Thursday, Friday, Saturday December 22nd to 28th'. Only Christmas day was exempt. It was closed.

In 1964 when the Sunshine Bingo Club had left the Corn Exchange for the Imperial Hall, Star Cinemas utilized the Corn Exchange to accommodate Star Bingo when the NAOS squeezed in a rehearsal on the Sunday in its limited time slot. This presentation was 'Bless the Bride'. The Society had set itself a huge challenge.

> "Costing £2,000 to stage it is the most expensive show the society has attempted. With nine scene changes, including four major sets, it presents a stage management problem of staggering proportions with 33 musical numbers in a score of formidable complexity. It taxes principals and chorus alike. It runs for about 3 hours and for most of the time the stage is literally crowded with people all dancing or otherwise about - playing croquet and tennis at one point."

> "The mind boggles at the thought that it all had to be put together with just one dress rehearsal at the Theatre. The energetic heroism of the backstage workers who had only this one opportunity to master all their bits and pieces deserves not to go unsung.

> It is not surprising that the scenery fell down during the dress rehearsal, nor that during the opening performance the lights came on while 'ghost dancers in a dream sequence were still scampering, bent double, off the stage, and two players in the game of tennis were disconcerted to find themselves without rackets. The wonder is that it could be done at all.'"

Through the next few productions Newark Amateur Operatic Society continued to suffer for their art but as the Mayor said at the Newark Amateur Operatic Society annual dinner in 1965:

> "You are doing a wonderful job and giving the people of Newark the chance to see shows which they would not otherwise be able to see without a long journey."

Mr F. Bellamy the Midlands Area representative of the National Operatic and Dramatic Association told members:

> "With good shows like the ones you have been putting on for the past few years you will get 'Full House' notices every night. 'Bless the Bride' sold 6,800 tickets and the Society have had 27,000 people to see the last few shows in the Palace."

The next productions of the Society at the Palace were 'South Pacific', 'Show Boat' and 'Annie Get Your Gun' and members of the Society took supporting roles in the Concert 'Gilbert and Sullivan For All' with D'Oyly

Carte Artistes Valerie Masterson, Philip Potter and Donald Adams presented at the Palace on the 24th April 1966.

However these eagerly awaited live shows at the Palace suddenly came to an end when as the Newark Advertiser announced on 26th August 1967 that

"like a deprived child Newark Operatic Society had nowhere to play. It is understandable that the Theatre owners who have had a thin time with films are cashing in on the Bingo bonanza. More evenings are to be made available for the patrons who are attracted by the Casino lure"

This final blow to live entertainment in Newark aroused the Newark populace who had previously crusaded

"a few years ago for a public hall for Newark. The public responded to an appeal for funds to build a hall, over £1,000 is in the bank but the idea has faded away. A few years ago Newark Town Council explored the prospects. Some enthusiasm was kindled but the project died. So does this latest edict, the notice to quit, evoke a touch of conscience among our governers of the town?" *Newark Advertiser* 26/8/67.

The original initial aims of Star Cinemas to provide live entertainment for the town, along with other diversifications to support the main bread winner, Cinema , foundered on the disasterous fall in cinema attendances. Walter Eckart bravely fought back by maximisation of catering facilities, Pop Concerts, international wrestling and provision of the best films. All his efforts however would have been fruitless without the advent of Bingo. This flood of enthusiasm for gambling occasioned by the changes in the Gaming Laws fundamentally changed Star Policy.

Walter Eckart died in 1964 and the Sons Derek and Rodney were not the devoted "Cinema People " like their father. The stagnant years were over with Bingo yielding profits of between 30%-40% despite close regulation by the Gaming board. Inevitably with cinemas almost empty the new direction led Star Cinemas to become by the end of 1971 Britain's biggest bingo and cinema empire. After 40 years as a private company it was finally letting in the public. A merger with the smaller British Lion organisation would allow the public to obtain 20% of the shares of the enlarged company. However Derek felt an element of necessity had produced this situation. "Quite honestly, I'd rather have kept it private".

Star went public solely because of the heavy burden of estate duty following the death of their father in 1964 and of their mother in 1969. They could have sold out to another company but were keen to keep running their own show. British Lion seemed to be a good way to get a quotation and broaden the Group's base at the same time. Their empire consisted of 150 Bingo halls (far more than anyone else) 107 cinemas, 6 discotheques and the Red Lion pub in Paris. Every week star attracts 750,000 paying customers with a business worth £10 million. Star's profits had roared up for £250,000 to 1½ million pounds from 1964 to 1971. Ailing cinema halls had been either shed or diversified into Silver Blades Ice rinks (now sold to Mecca) or Star excels at converting cinemas to bingo cum social clubs quickly and cheaply and it was one of the first to see the sense in combining mini cinemas and bingo clubs in the same building.

By 1971 it has dozens of Cinema bingo splits, Studio cinemas and twin cinemas. On average it adds 3 new units every fortnight. It was logical therefore that the vast profits on gambling should be maximised and led in 1968 to the Palace becoming exclusively a Bingo Hall.

4.   Save The Palace

However just a couple of months after the 1967 expelling of the Newark Operatic Society from the Palace, the theatre had a hit film. By special permission of Nottinghamshire County Council the complete and unabridged version of James Joyce's Ulysses was passed for public exhibition in Newark. Presumably the Palace was chosen because of the film's eroticism or reputation of eroticism. A postal booking form was placed in the *Advertiser* and an advance booking office set up in the Palace. Briefly every moment that was not Bingo was Ulysses: Sunday 4.15 p.m., Monday, Tuesday and Thursday 2.45 p.m. & 8 p.m., Saturdays 2.45, 5.30, 8.20. Matinee Wednesday & Friday 2.45 p.m. and 8 p.m. Saturdays 2.45 p.m., 5.30 p.m. and 8.20 p.m. Matinees Wednesday and Friday 2.45 p.m., Late show Friday 10.30 p.m. Prices were 10/6d - 6/6d. A report says that this classic film ran for three weeks at about 500 patrons per night. "Hundreds came by coaches on works outings from Leeds, Loughborough and Derby".

On the 1st September 1968 Bingo was established for 7 nights a week. The only films to be shown were from 24/5/69 to 13/12/69 when a weekly Saturday afternoon family matinee was sandwiched between

Bingo sessions.

The Newark Amateur Operatic Society had soldiered on without the Palace stage at other venues including the unsuitable shallow stage at the Savoy. Every local newspaper advertised live entertainment at venues everywhere except Newark. The discontent surfaced finally with a crowded meeting in the town hall in February 1969 with the aim of providing a purpose built Arts Centre to serve the local populace. Over previous years many hopeful possibilities had been fruitlessly high-lighted and came to nothing. But signs looked good as 350 delegates from Newark and Southwell overfilled the ballroom. A committee was set up and the Arts and Leisure Association for Newark and district was launched. However by January 1971 nothing effective had been done.

At the first Annual General meeting two years after the launch the Newark and District Arts and Leisure Association nearly died. Only 19 people attended the meeting in Newark Preparatory School and set about finding a new Chairman, Secretary and Treasurer who had all resigned after the 1969 launch. However by this time other bodies had been active. At the Silver Jubilee dinner of the Newark Music Club in March 1970 the Mayor of Newark Mr Leslie Carswell said "I think that when we can fill the parish church on 2 occasions does it not emphasise more than ever the need for a public hall fitting for Newark"? "A larger hall would enable better concerts to be given and the hall could easily be filled. After all £196 was raised and handed over to the Save the Children Fund as a result of the Christmas concerts in the church."

Out of the blue on 16th January 1971 in the *Newark Advertiser* was the front page headline "Town may buy Theatre". "On Thursday 14th January a spokesman for Star Holdings of Leeds, which owns the Palace, said the Council had expressed an interest in acquiring it. We have received an enquiry from the Town Council as to whether we would be interested in selling the Palace. We have sent an appropriate reply to the effect that the Palace could be sold to them. But the Palace is not on the market generally".

What a surge of speculation this announcement must have caused. The *Advertiser's* reporter found the Council quite reticent but the Council official although declining any comment stated "This is still with one of the Council's committees. We do not publicise details of any property in connection with which the Corporation may be negotiating".

Star Cinema's were also anxious to quell rumours that there was no plans to replace the Savoy with a first floor cinema over a ground floor supermarket or arcade.

However as the avowed policy of Star Cinema's was to rationalize their properties it is not surprising that the Palace may have looked somewhat surplus to requirements when the Savoy building was modern, on a prime site and capable of being adapted into a studio multi cinema or a bingo/cinema split or even cinema/bingo/supermarket. Whereas the huge Palace wore a dowdy look and the *Advertiser* reported on 13th February 1971 that "except for sessions on Friday's and Sunday's attendances at the Palace Bingo Club have been falling off for some months."

"The Council minutes published Thursday 28th January confirmed that the owners Star Associated Holdings Ltd have offered to sell it to the Council. Councillor Chris Grant had a few days before the Council meeting persauded NADALA to continue and revive its interest in maintaining contact between the Arts and Sports associations of the town and the authorities, despite the opening of the Grove Sports Centre at Balderton. Now Councillor Grant preparatory to the next meeting of the Council had offered to make a feasibility study. On Monday 1st February the Council will be asked to accept his offer which could result in the Council buying the Palace. Councillor Grant expects some opposition to the idea but hopes the Council will not deny the town a facility he believes many people think it needs.

The Council accepted Councillor Grant's offer to produce a feasibility study.

In May a disturbing statement on the position of the Amateur Operatic Society by its Chairman Councillor Chris Grant on the occasion of the annual dinner at the beginning of May placed a further obligation upon the Council to save the Palace.

"Newark's 35 year old Amateur Operatic Society could cease to exist in two or three months. Councillor Grant 'fears that because the Society has nowhere to stage its productions it will disintegrate as members interest flags'. After the current production of the Mikardo and an invitation to support Gilbert and Sullivan Ltd in a production of Yeoman of the Guard at Nottingham Castle 'without a home and without an annual production the society will decline and quickly talented members will go elsewhere'. If this Society dies as the Technical College Drama Group has done a piece of Newark will die too."

The feasibility study report for which the Council had agreed to defer a decision was completed before the end of June. Under the chairmanship of Councillor Grant were Mr John Oldham and Mr Roger Kemp of Newark Civic Trust, Mr John Docherty Chairman of Newark and District Arts and Leisure Association (NADALA), Mr George Bennett vice president of Newark Amateur Operatic Society and Doctor Victor Twyman Chairman of Newark Music Club.

This highly experienced group produced a first class report which critics would find difficult to either oppose or fault. Its conclusion was

"that Newark and district is particularly fortunate to have the opportunity of acquiring a building which in so many ways, fulfils the needs which have been voiced for so long at a price which is a small fraction of the £150,000 that a new building of similar size would cost.

The road so far has been paved with lost opportunities, shelved schemes, dashed hopes and frustrated aspirations. Now there is a chance to do something about it. True it will cost a certain amount of money, but it is impossible to measure the benefits of such an enterprise in purely financial terms.

What is needed now is the vision and imagination to see the Palace as an asset which the town and district cannot afford to lose and a vigorous effort by everyone concerned to ensure that its potential is fully realised."

This study is invaluable to a researcher. No detailed report of the condition of the building had been made since a few weeks before the Palace opened in 1920. Despite over 50 years of wear

"the building is in good condition structurally. The sixty foot span slated roofs over the auditorium and fly tower are almost as good today as when built. Such faults and defects which the building may have arise from the original design, ordinary wear and tear, neglect of decoration and finishings and old fashioned toilet facilities. Design faults include the obtrusive columns in the stalls and poorly planned dressing rooms in the semi basement under the stage. The buildings most obvious defect is its dowdy decorative condition internally and externally.

It looks unattractive and many of the finishes and furnishings are in need of repair and renewal. A limited number of seats need replacing or recovering. The heating system is reasonably efficient and although the boiler is solid fuel hand fired it appears to be in good order. The electrical system has been altered and adapted over the years. The front of the building facing Appleton Gate incorporates two shops which are at present let and used for the sale of frozen foods and wines and spirits. At the back of the main building is a range of single storey buildings which contains the boiler room, a store and large workshop. In addition there is a strip of land 40 ft deep by 90 ft wide at present used as a motor vehicle repair yard with access from the road at the side of the theatre."

On Monday 26 July 1971 the council's response to the feasibilty study was to unanimously pass three resolutions:

"1) That a negotiating committee, consisting of the Mayor of Newark, Councillor Richard Lamb, Councillor Tim Healey and Councillor Robert Wilkinson, be appointed to negotiate with Star Cinemas an option to purchase the property.

2) That the Mayor be requested to approach the Chairman of Newark and Southwell Rural District Councils with a view to sponsoring a joint public appeal towards the purchase and development of the Palace Theatre as a leisure centre.

3) That Newark and Southwell Rural District Councils be approached with a view to setting up a joint committee to explore the possibility of developing the Palace as a leisure centre to be administered by a board of trustees."

Chiel's comments in the Advertiser were euphoric:-

"Hoist the flag on Newark Town Hall. At a special meeting of the town council on Monday members favoured the purchase of the Palace Theatre if the terms are right. It was the longest meeting for years and was attended by a record number of the general public; more onlookers than councillors and some had to stand. The unanimity of the Council was above politics. The Town Council pulled together on Monday for the good of the people.

Now let the people pull together and show they are prepared to work - and pay for what they want."

At a crowded lively meeting at the Town Hall, on the 2nd September 1971, it was unanimously agreed that:-

a steering committee with power to coopt should launch an appeal to raise £30,000 to buy the theatre. The proposals and suggestions were unanimously accepted by the meeting and almost immediately Mrs Doris Bullock unofficially opened the appeal fund with a personal donation of £50. Councillor Alan Hine announced that his brother Dr Denys Hine during whose mayoralty a fund was launched for a public hall for Newark had told him the fund now stood at £2,000 which he hoped the fund committee would pass on to the organisers of the Palace appeal.

Councillor Leslie Carswell said after the meeting that the appeal would be launched officially when the negotiating committee had successfully negotiated an option to purchase with Star Associated Holdings Ltd of Leeds owners of the Palace in accordance with the town council's resolution of July 26th.

Mr George Bennett said "We have talked about having a public hall four times. We always talk. Let us have some enthusiasm." The mayor replied, "that is why I have called this meeting this evening. Many people have made sacrifices to come to it. I have sacrificed something because it happens to be my wedding anniversary." "Congratulations" said Mr Bennett whose wishes were echoed by the meeting.

On 19th October the Council negotiators came face to face for the first time with a Star representative, Company Secretary Mr Frank Cox. The outcome will be reported back to the Council. However Star Cinemas decided on 6th November to put the Palace on the open market at a price of £30,000 in November as it negotiated a £20 million tie up with British Lion Holdings. The purchase price seemed high to the Council negotiaters. Councillor Healey said on 4th November 1971:

> "I think £30,000 is more than anyone will pay. The land is not worth that alone and the building would cost an enormous amount to convert. So it is virtually a one purpose building and who apart from us wants a theatre in Newark."

In January 1972 crucial talks were held at the Palace. The Council negotiating team offered £20,000 for the Palace. Star Cinemas compromised at £25,000. The negotiating team were to liaise with the appeal's committee. The *Advertiser* announced on the front page 12th February 1972

> "Star say Yes on Palace."
> "The owners of the Palace Star Associated Holdings have accepted a £25,000 bid put in by Newark's three man negotiating committee and granted a six month option to buy.
> Mr Frank Cox Star's Company Secretary said the reasons for Newark asking for only an option to buy were appreciated by Star: At the same time it will do our business at the Palace harm if it is to be constantly advertised that the premises are likely to be taken over by the Corporation. Star also stipulated that any publicity should make it known that the Bingo Club at the Palace will be transferred to the Savoy Cinema in Middlegate.
> The people of Newark area have now six months to raise £25,000 to buy the Palace Theatre for an Arts and Leisure Centre."

From the earliest days of The Palace Theatre opening, charity performances always received excellent support, so it was with the fund to buy the Palace for an arts centre and leisure centre.

Prior to the official launch monies rolled in. On 14th April Mr Leslie Carswell now Deputy Mayor and Chairman of the executive concerned with raising money to establish the Palace Theatre apologised at the lateness in launching the appeal. He explained that it was not until February that an option to purchase was agreed by Star Holdings. Since

> "much spade work had to be done. The executive committee had accepted that the whole concept was far bigger than was ever envisaged at the initial public meeting in June of last year". "We must have enough money to franchise the Palace. We must in addition have sufficient money to ensure that the project can prosper in smooth water". "Already a very acceptable sum has been given by keen and enthusiastic supporters." He concluded that "this chance is one that will never occur again in our lifetime. We cannot afford to fail and I am certain with all the help forthcoming we will not fail."

The other large item in the same edition of the *Advertiser* announced that work will begin next week on a multi thousand pound project to create a new four cinema luxury cinema complex out of the Savoy by the Star Group of Companies.

On the 15th July the appeal was finally launched for £70,000. By 24th August the appeal fund had reached £22,388 excluding £15,000 from the Town Council which was to pay for the conversion of the building. "In hard cash we have £11,000" said Mr Carswell "the rest is from covenants - but through the good offices of an anonymous benefactor who has been kind enough to provide us with a bridging loan the actual purchase money is virtually available. "We are now entering phase 2 to raise the balance of £32,400.

Finally in September the front page of the *Newark Advertiser* declared

"The Newark and Notts Arts and Leisure Centre appeal fund has this week topped the £25,000 purchase price of the Palace Theatre and two rural local authorities have been asked to make grants or loans towards the funds target of £70,000. With the £15,000 contribution from the borough the fun now exceeds £40,000.

As the purchase money was raised and the fund still accumulating healthily it was decided to appoint a centre director. The Palace was saved and in business.As the *Advertiser* heading ran "CURTAIN UP".

SUBSCRIBERS TO "THE PALACE YEARS"

Mr R.G. Abraham
Michael C. Anderson
Dr M.H. Anderton
Don Atherton
Mrs J. Bailey
Mr & Mrs G.J. Bakker
Dave Baliol-Key
Jill & Mick Ball
Philip Ball
Tom Bickley
Alexander Bisset
Patricia Black
Brian Bland
John Briggs
Dorothy Britton
A. Brooke
Eric Broomhead
J.W. Bullimore
Mr P.A. Burnett
M.J. Burn-Murdoch
Mr R. Carr
S.J. Cave
Mr G.O. Chandler
Leon Charlesworth
Brien Chitty
Mrs M. Clayton
Elaine Coates
Yvonne Cockayne
J. Cook
E.M. Cooke
Vina Cooke
Roland Cope
Mrs P. Coyne
Mrs P. Cull
John R. Davies
Betty & Malcolm Dawes
Ray & Gillian Dicks
Maureen & Vincent Dobson
Mr R.H. Edlin
R. Fawcett
June & Derrick Fielden
Bill Flisher
Kelly Forrest
Sue Foster
Margaret Gaughan

Mr F. Gelder
D.C. Ghent
Ann Gilbert
M.J. Gill
K. Heather Greensmith
Mr J.T. Griffin
Mrs H. Hage
Mrs G.E. Hall
Tim Hambling
Mr D.A. Hammond
Mrs G. Hatcher
Mrs M. Henry
Mr E. Holden
Peter & Pat Holland
Martin Holloway
David Holmes
Stephanie Hopkinson
Patrick Howell
James Howlett & Sharon Jones
Frances Hughes
June Hunt
J.A. Instone
Mrs C.S. Johnson
Miss C.A. Jones
Mrs G.E. Jones
Ms V.A. Jones
Mr P.B. Jowett
Barbara Keegan
John Kennedy
Paul J. Kent
J.C. King
Mr A.C.K. Lawrence
E.W. Leslie
Rod Little
Nick Lumley
Mr A. McCarroll
Mrs L. McKenzie
Mr E.W. Marr
A.J. Marriot
C.R. Marshall
Mr & Mrs D.J. Mellors
A. Miles
Nerissa Moore
J.W. Molloson
Audrey Noble

Leslie Orton
Lady Osborn
Miss Roma Parlby
Mrs Gerda Pinkney
David Piper
Mr I.D. Plaskett
Kevin Porter
T.R. & D. Quarrington
Gladys & Vernon Radcliffe
Jack Reading
Mr C.W. Redwood
Mrs A. Riley
A.C. Roberts
Mrs J.R. Roe
Mrs J.A. Rushforth
T.W. Seaton
Iris Shepley
Ned Sherrin
Mr R. Slack
Brian W. Smith
I.D. Smith
Mrs K.A. Smith
Mrs B. Stubbens
Brenda Taylor
Chris Thursby
James L. Todd
Mrs B.A. Tuffee
Wendy & Ken Turk
Miss A. Twitchett
Mr R.E. Tyers
Mr R.A. Vinnicombe
James Robert Waddell
Art Walker
M. Walton
Mr T. Warner
Mr M.D. Weston
E.A. Whistler
Mr M.F. & Mrs M. Whiting
Mrs W.E. Wilde
Sara Williams
Mrs Sheila Williams
Mr David C. Wood
Gillian Wright

119